Lebendiges Englisch 2

Arbeitsbuch und Grammatik

von Hans G. Hoffmann

Max Hueber Verlag

LEBENDIGES ENGLISCH 2
Ein moderner Sprachkurs für Schule, Beruf und Weiterbildung
Arbeitsbuch und Grammatik von Hans G. Hoffmann

Materialbeschaffung und Recherchen: Brigitte Hoffmann
Sprachliche Durchsicht und Beratung: Hilary Heltay, Iris Owen
Verlagsredaktion: John Stevens
Umschlagentwurf und Layout: Karl Schaumann

Redaktionsschluß der 1. Auflage: Mai 1979

Für die Genehmigung zum Abdruck von Copyright-Material dankt der Verlag den folgenden Personen bzw. Institutionen:

Australian Tourist Agency: Foto S. 39
Hans G. Hoffmann (Windeck): Foto S. 52
Phelps & Thompson Camera Press (London): Foto S. 34
Punch/Werner Lüning (Lübeck): Punch-Zeichnungen S. 4, 6, 8, 9, 13, 16, 17, 18, 20, 23, 25, 26, 27, 29, 33, 35, 36, 38, 45, 48, 50, 56, 70, 73, 75, 76, 82, 84, 94, 95, 105, 118, 122, 124, 133, 135, 145, 147, 149, 152

---

1. Auflage

3. 2. 1. | Die letzten Ziffern
1983 82 81 80 79 | bezeichnen Zahl und Jahr des Druckes.
Alle Drucke dieser Auflage können nebeneinander benutzt werden.

Satz und Druck: Georg Appl, Wemding · Printed in Germany
ISBN 3–19–03.2192–2

Inhaltsverzeichnis

1

1N Infinitiv zum Ausdruck des Zwecks

Make sentences as in the examples.

Why did he ring them? – He wanted to make an appointment. He rang them to make an appointment.
Why did he meet Mr Stewart? – He wanted to discuss the North Sea project. He met Mr Stewart to discuss the North Sea project.

a. Why did they form a chain? – They wanted to pour water over the whale.
b. Why did they stop in Orpington? – They wanted to visit the Garnetts.
c. Why did he go out? – He wanted to get some exercise.
d. Why did she go to London? – She wanted to take an English course.
e. Why did he write to them? – He wanted to thank them for their present.
f. Why did she go to the station? – She wanted to meet Brian.
g. Why did she buy the newspapers? – She wanted to have something to read on the plane.

1O Look forward to doing something

You are going to London next week. Say what you are looking forward to doing there.

. . . eat a chicken curry at an Indian restaurant in Soho I'm looking forward to eating a chicken curry at an Indian restaurant in Soho.

"I'm looking forward to sitting in my armchair and reading a good book."

. . . meet Jane and Frank again
. . . see some good new plays at the theatre
. . . hear a concert at the Royal Festival Hall
. . . take pictures of the sights of London
. . . do some shopping in Oxford Street and Regent Street
. . . drink beer and play darts in a riverside pub

1P **Infinitiv oder -ing-Form?**

Put in the correct forms of the verbs in brackets.

At the moment he is busy (plan) his trip to Glasgow.
At the moment he is busy planning his trip to Glasgow.

I don't often manage (watch) television in the evenings.
I don't often manage to watch television in the evenings.

a. I think it's my turn (buy) drinks now. b. It was a particular pleasure for me (come) to your home. c. Wouldn't you like (go) back to work in the factory? d. I'd like (pick) up my ticket. e. He doesn't like (have) to work on Bank Holidays. f. Would you mind (answer) a few questions? g. The best way (travel) is (walk). h. The most popular pastime for both sexes is (watch) television. i. You seem (think) that harsh penalties are the best means (reduce) crime. j. He began (earn) his living at the age of eleven. k. She started (learn) English five years ago. l. I remember (learn) a poem by Housman at school. m. We stopped (pay) a short visit to the place where my wife was born. n. (Watch) television can harm the development of young children.

1Q **Indirekte Rede** (→ GIV20)

Change the following sentences as in the examples.

"I *have* a meeting at 8.30."
What did she say? – She said she *had* a meeting at 8.30.

"I*'ll* meet her at the airport."
What did he say? – He said he*'d* (= he *would*) meet her at the airport.

a. "I *have* to be there at six o'clock."
What did she say?

b. "We always *have* a spare bed for Bill."
What did they say?

c. "I *live* in a suburb of London."
What did she say?

d. "We*'re* interested in the project."
What did they say?

e. "My plane *arrives* at 18.25."
What did he say?

f. "I*'ll* be staying with friends."
What did he say?

g. "I*'ll* send it under separate cover."
What did he say?

h. "That *won't* be necessary."
What did he say?

1R **Aktiv und Passiv** (→ GIV21)

Aktiv:	You'**ll have to make** an appointment.
Passiv:	An appointment **will have to be made.**
Aktiv:	We'**ll have to discuss** the details of the North Sea project.
Passiv:	The details of the North Sea project **will have to be discussed.**

Change these sentences as in the examples.

a. You'll have to book seats early.
b. You'll have to arrange accommodation.
c. You'll have to translate this letter.
d. We'll have to cancel our reservation at Brown's Hotel.
e. You'll have to send these letters today.
f. We'll have to get the texts for the new catalogue ready.

"It'll have to be repaired."

1S **On the phone**

Taylor here. / Taylor speaking.	*Hier ist / spricht Taylor.*
Hello, (this is) Brian Taylor speaking.	*Hallo, hier spricht . . .*
Could you put me through to Mr Smith.	*Könnten Sie mich mit . . . verbinden.*
Can I speak to Mr Smith, please.	*Kann ich bitte Herrn . . . sprechen.*
Hold the line, please.	*Bleiben Sie bitte am Apparat.*
Hold on a moment.	*Bleiben Sie einen Augenblick am Apparat.*
Thank you / Thanks for calling / ringing.	*Danke für den Anruf.*

1T **Modale Hilfsverben** (→ GIII41 ff.)

Please translate.

a. Könnten Sie mich bitte mit dem Flugscheinschalter verbinden. b. Es könnte schlimmer sein. c. Wie konnte sie mir das antun? d. Er könnte denken, daß wir Angst vor ihm haben. e. Wollen wir zehn Uhr sagen? f. Was wollen wir heute abend machen? g. Die Sitzung dürfte / müßte bis 9.30 (Uhr) vorüber sein. h. (Das) Rauchen sollte hier nicht erlaubt sein. i. Das hätte nicht passieren dürfen.

1U **Ausdrücke mit Präpositionen**

Prägen Sie sich die folgenden Ausdrücke mit Präpositionen gut ein.

at arrive **at** Glasgow Airport (but: **in** Glasgow) *am Flughafen Glasgow ankommen* **at** a pinch *zur Not / notfalls*	**to** he talked **to** Shirley *er sprach mit S.* in reply **to** your letter *in Beantwortung Ihres Schreibens* his visit **to** Glasgow *sein Besuch in Glasgow*
by is it all right **by** you? *ist es dir recht?*	**under** **under** separate cover *mit getrennter Post*
on **on** the Thursday morning (but: **in** the morning) *am Donnerstag morgen*	**with** stay **with** friends *bei Freunden wohnen* have a job **with** a company *bei einer Firma beschäftigt sein*

1V **Dictation exercise**

Hören Sie das Diktat vom Tonband und schreiben Sie dabei diejenigen Wörter nieder, die im folgenden Diktattext fehlen.

______ Brian and Shirley,

______ a short note to let you ______ that I got back ______. The ______ was very ______ and, as ______, both Rita and our dog, Bello, were waiting for me at the airport.

______ again many thanks for ______ me stay with you. I ______ every minute of the time we ______ together.

We hope you'll ______ your word and visit us on your way ______ during the summer ______.

______ from Rita. And please give my ______ to the boys.

Yours ever,

Günter

1W **Put in: about, at, by, during, in, of, on, through, to, with.**

a. Could you put me . . . . . to Mr Stewart's office, please. b. We're planning to meet . . . . . the second half of January to discuss the project. c. The meeting should be over . . . . . 9.30 at the latest. d. I'll probably be staying . . . . . friends . . . . . a suburb . . . . . Glasgow. e. I look forward . . . . . seeing you . . . . . the airport. f. He has a well-paid job . . . . . Stewart & Son . . . . . Glasgow. g. Do you have any questions . . . . . the details . . . . . the trip? h. What flight will you arrive . . . . . ? i. Who will you be met . . . . . ? j. Will it be all right . . . . . you if he comes . . . . . the Thursday evening? k. . . . . . a pinch I could pick it up there . . . . . my next visit . . . . . Glasgow.

"By flying Concorde you can do the whole of Europe in three days instead of the usual four."

2H **Futur: Verlaufsform zum Ausdruck der Zukunft** (→ 1M)

We **are having** a little party the weekend after next.
When **are** you **leaving?**
We **are leaving** for a two-week holiday on May 21st.

Wird die Verlaufsform zum Ausdruck zukünftiger Handlungen gebraucht, so steht sie in der Regel in Verbindung mit einer Zeitbestimmung der Zukunft (*the weekend after next, May 21st* etc.) oder dem Fragewort *when.*

Make sentences as in the example.

I / fly / to Glasgow tomorrow afternoon I'm flying to Glasgow tomorrow afternoon.
When / you / have / your meeting with Mr Stewart When are you having your meeting with Mr Stewart?

a. my daughter / get / married in January
b. we / go / to a concert at the Royal Festival Hall tonight
c. Gerry / come / to see us this afternoon
d. when / you / go / to Malta
e. we / spend / the summer holidays in Swanage this year
f. when / we / arrive / at Heathrow
g. the bar / close / in a few minutes
h. the Prime Minister / visit / France at the end of this month
i. when / you / move / into your new house
j. it's Friday, so we / have / fish for dinner today
k. what / you / do / tomorrow
l. we / watch / television this evening

"We're opening a new branch in Accra next month."

2I Bedingungssätze

Unterscheiden Sie die beiden folgenden Grundtypen des Bedingungssatzes (zum dritten Grundtyp → 13H).

Typ 1

If-Satz: **Präsens**	Hauptsatz: **will** / **won't** + Infinitiv
If you **go** by train,	you **will** / **won't** get there in two hours.

Typ 2

If-Satz: **Vergangenheitsform**	Hauptsatz: **would(n't)** + Infinitiv
If you **went** by train,	you **would(n't)** get there in two hours.

Put in will / 'll or would / 'd.

a. If you leave at 15.30 from St Pancras, you ..... arrive in Nottingham at 18.17.
b. If it's too big for the envelope, we ..... send it under separate cover.
c. If I was a toolmaker, I ..... be earning about £65 a week.
d. I'm sure you ..... find something for her if you go to Macy's.
e. I ..... buy him a drink if I were you – he gets aggressive when he's sober.
f. Alf Garnett ..... not like it if a black moved in next door.
g. If you go to the White Horse, you ..... have a lot of fun.
h. It ..... not be so cheap if it wasn't a package holiday.

2J Put in the correct forms of the words in brackets.

a. If the plane (arrive) at half past six, we'll be at your place at half past seven. b. If the brewery (give) me free beer for the rest of my life, I wouldn't drink more than I do now. c. If I (win) £50,000 on the football pools, I would start a business of my own. d. If this dog (do not) find a new owner, it will have to be destroyed. e. We would come to your party if we (be not) going to be away on that date. f. If you (go) on foot, you'll meet interesting people along the road. g. We wouldn't be any better off if we (have) a business of our own. h. I'd open the windows if they (be not) sealed.

2K **Zum englischen Zeitengebrauch** (→ GIV17)

Handlung fand in der Vergangenheit statt	(Ohne Zeitbestimmung) I **have** (just) **found** a splendid book for you. (Mit Zeitbestimmung) I **found** a splendid book (at Foyle's) yesterday.
Handlung erstreckt sich aus der Vergangenh. in die Gegenw.	They **have been** married for ten years (now). She **has been living** with him for five years (now).
Gegenwart	My goodness, how the time **flies!** **I'm dying** of heat.
Handlung findet in der Zukunft statt	(Will) We **will** / **We'll be** away at the time of your wedding anniversary. (Be + -ing) We **are having** a little party on Saturday. (Will be + -ing) I **will** / **I'll be arriving** at Glasgow Airport at 18.25. (Be going to) We **are going to build** more hospitals. (Präsens) Our train **leaves** at 16.50.

Please complete.

a. I (visit) Glasgow next January.
I (visit) Glasgow last October.

b. The Taylors (live) in Glasgow for about ten years now. They (move) to Glasgow about ten years ago.

c. We (just receive) your letter of April 10. We (receive) your letter yesterday. We (get) dozens of such letters every day.

d. Carol and Alan (be) married for over ten years now. They (get) married ten years ago. Their marriage (be) very happy so far. –
When (Rita and Brian get) married? Next year?

e. I (never see) this shop before.
How long (it be) here?
Only since last week. It (be) opened last Wednesday.
It's a discount bookshop which (sell) books at half their normal price.

f. This book looks very interesting. Where (you buy) it? – I (buy) it at Foyle's. – Foyle's? That's the big bookshop in Charing Cross Road, isn't it? I (always buy) my books at Dillon's in Malet Street.

g. Hatchard's, London's oldest bookshop, (be) at 187 Piccadilly since 1767.

h. (You be) free on the morning of the 20th? – No, not really. I (have) a meeting at my office at 8.30. – When do you think the meeting (be) over? – Well, the last time that man (come) to see me he (stay) till lunch.

i. I (play) a lot of football when I (be) young. Nowadays I (never play) football. I (play) tennis ever since I (give up) football. – Where's John? – He (play) tennis. He (play) tennis since about two o'clock.

2L **Please complete.**

a. About three weeks ago we (place) an order for £265 worth of goods.
The goods we (order) three weeks ago (not arrive) yet.
Please let us know when you (send off) the goods we (order) three weeks ago.
The goods you (order) on March 7 (send off) within the next three days.

b. My holiday (start) the day after tomorrow.
Oh, how nice. Where (you go)?
To America. A tour of the East Coast, starting in Boston. We (fly) from Heathrow. The flight (take) about seven hours. I must be going now. My wife (wait) for me.

2M **Objektsätze** (→ GIII54)

Add "do you think", as in the examples.

What sort of place is it? What sort of place do you think it is?
Why does Stephen mention the young Swedish couple? Why do you think Stephen mentions the young Swedish couple?

a. How old is he? b. When was this book published? c. Where do you get better service – in a very large store or in a small shop? d. Why does that happen? e. How did he usually pass the day? f. Where did he stay when he was in Glasgow? g. Why did he visit them? h. Why don't they want to get married?

2N **Modale Hilfsverben** (→ GIII41 ff.) – **Please translate.**

a. Könnten wir auch um acht kommen? b. Wir würden uns so freuen, wenn ihr kommen könntet. c. Carl Sandburgs Vater konnte seinen eigenen Namen nicht schreiben. d. Als er das Badezimmer verlassen wollte, stellte er fest, daß er die Tür nicht öffnen konnte. e. Werdet ihr beide kommen können? f. Er wird ohne mich auskommen müssen, während ich weg bin. g. Muß man die Plätze im voraus buchen? h. Ich weiß nicht, warum ich heiraten sollte. i. Ich sollte die Nacht in einem Hotel in der Nähe des Flughafens verbringen ("es war so vorgesehen").

Prägen Sie sich die folgenden Ausdrücke mit Präpositionen gut ein.

at
late **at** night *spätabends*
look **at** the map *auf die Landkarte schauen*
at the very last moment
im allerletzten Augenblick

by
invitation **by** telephone
telefonische Einladung

for
he's been living there **for** five years
er lebt seit fünf Jahren dort

of
die **of** heat
vor Hitze sterben

on
go **on** foot *zu Fuß gehen*
win £50,000 **on** the football pools
50000 Pfund im Fußballtoto gewinnen
I have no money **on** me
ich habe kein Geld bei mir
the map **on** the left
die linksstehende / nebenstehende Karte
I'll be away **on** that date
zu diesem Zeitpunkt werde ich verreist sein
hearty congratulations **on** your wedding anniversary! *herzliche Glückwünsche zu eurem Hochzeitstag!*

in
he's **in** love *er ist verliebt*
a house **in** the country
ein Haus auf dem Lande
get to the airport **in** time
rechtzeitig zum Flughafen kommen

to
an invitation **to** dinner
eine Einladung zum Essen
she showed him **to** his seat
sie führte ihn zu seinem Platz

"What, you haven't got any money on you?"

2P **Put in: about, at, by, for, of, on, since, to.**

a. What do you think . . . . . this letter here? Isn't it strange? b. He says he won the money . . . . . the football pools. c. When are Ann and Stephen leaving . . . . . Malta? d. Congratulations . . . . . winning the first prize! e. They've been living in Portland Drive . . . . . three years now. f. Is there a restaurant car . . . . . the eleven-oh-five to Nottingham? g. Carol and Alan are celebrating their tenth wedding anniversary . . . . . Saturday 28th and have asked us to join them . . . . . dinner. h. I haven't seen them . . . . . my last visit . . . . . Nuneaton. i. If you look . . . . . the map, you'll find that Nuneaton is east . . . . . Birmingham. j. I'm afraid I have no money . . . . . me . . . . . the moment. k. . . . . . arriving late at night . . . . . their hotel they were told that their room had been given . . . . . someone else. l. I usually go . . . . . bus, but . . . . . a day like this I prefer to go . . . . . foot.

2Q **Dictation exercise**

Hören Sie das Diktat vom Tonband und schreiben Sie dabei diejenigen Wörter nieder, die im folgenden Diktattext fehlen.

Dear Carol and Alan,

______ you very much for the ______ dinner yesterday. We both enjoyed it a lot.

It was ______ to meet so many old ______ again, and we ______ enjoyed looking at the film taken of your wedding ten years ago.

It's a ______ Ann and Stephen ______ come. It ______ have been nice to see them again after all these years.

If you ______ ever come to our part of the ______, you must look us up.

If you can bring the ______, so much the better. Tell them ______ find lots of ______ here: a dog and two cats, ______, some cows, and even a pony to ______ on. There are also ______ to play in and a lake not too far away where they ______ go ______ or boating.

All good ______,

Yours ever,

John and Sandra

3I **Ask questions with what, what . . . like, when, where, why, and how.**

Hand-made glass objects are suitable souvenirs to bring home from Malta. *What* are suitable souvenirs to bring home from Malta?
She brought *some beautiful lace* from Malta. *What* did she bring from Malta?
The water of the Mediterranean is *warm and clear.* *What* is the water of the Mediterranean *like*?

a. The languages spoken in Malta are *Maltese and English.*
b. *The fact that it is an English-speaking country* makes Malta particularly attractive to students of English.
c. Their courier told them about *their rooms, sporting and recreation facilities, and so on.*
d. Malta is surrounded by *the Mediterranean* Sea.
e. Malta's winter is *short and mild.*
f. The weather was *glorious.*
g. She got here *by plane.*
h. They spend most of the day *sunbathing, swimming, and playing tennis.*
i. The next group of tourists arrives *tomorrow afternoon.*
j. Malta became independent from Britain *in 1964.*
k. They stayed *at a nice little hotel in Gozo.*
l. They won't be able to come *because they will be away.*

3J **Put in some or any.**

a. Did you bring . . . . . souvenirs from Malta? – Yes, we brought . . . . .thing for the children. b. I'm afraid I didn't lose . . . . . weight in Malta. The food was too good. c. I think I lost . . . . . weight when I was in hospital. d. We've still got . . . . . tickets left, if you're interested. e. My wife and I are both working, so we don't want . . . . . children for the time being. f. We haven't had . . . . . complaints so far. Are you sure? Didn't we have . . . . . about the new model RT-10? g. I'm sure the air conditioning will make . . . . . difference. h. It won't make . . . . . difference whether you go by car or by train. i. Our dog has never bitten . . . . .body. j. When a dog bites . . . . .body, it's often the person's own fault. k. Will there be . . . . .body waiting for us at the airport when we arrive? l. (*Aufforderung:*) Why don't you get yourself . . . . .thing to drink?

3K **Steigerung: Komparativ** (→ LE1 22F–22H)

The average woman's working week is ten hours (long) than the average man's. The average woman's working week is ten hours longer than the average man's.

a. The water was (warm) than I had expected. b. A holiday at the seaside is (nice) than a holiday in the mountains. c. This job is much (interesting) than my last one. d. The Prime Minister is always (optimistic) than the experts. e. Are you (well) off now than you were in your old job? f. Are American-made programmes (good) or (bad) than programmes made in this country? g. He's right (often) than he's wrong. h. Writing a poem is (difficult) than writing a routine business letter. i. He never has (much) than $2^1/_2$ pints at the pub. j. The average woman still earns much (little) than the average man. k. Working on the assembly line is much (boring and tiring) than working in a shop.

3L **Steigerung: Superlativ** (→ LE1 23G)

Malta has Europe's (long) summer and (mild) winter. Malta has Europe's longest summer and mildest winter.

"They may be happily married, but they're the most boring people I've ever met."

a. Love seems to be the (swift) but is in fact the (slow) of all growths. b. In Malta, August is the (hot), December the (wet), and July the (dry) month of the year. c. This is the (happy) day of my life. d. The (popular) pastime for both sexes is watching television. e. The (intelligent) animal is the chimpanzee. f. The Savoy is one of the (good) hotels in London. g. This is one of the (bad) films / (big) dogs I've ever seen. h. The language with the (many) words is English. i. Giving the boy a bed and breakfast is the (little) we can do for him.

3M Substantivierung des Verbs: -ing-Konstruktion als Subjekt

> (Das) Einkaufen in den überfüllten Straßen u. Märkten macht großen Spaß.
> Shopping in the crowded streets and markets is great fun.

Please translate.

a. (Das) Umherfahren ist einfach und billig: mit dem Bus, mit dem Taxi oder mit der Pferdedroschke.
b. (Das) Rauchen ist schlecht für die Gesundheit.
c. (Das) Fernsehen kann bei kleinen Kindern der Entwicklung schaden.
d. (Das) Arbeiten am Fließband ist sehr ermüdend.
e. Tanzen ist etwas, was ich hasse.
f. In diesem Hotel ist jeden Abend Tanz.
g. In einem Restaurant zu essen ist teurer, als zu Hause zu essen.
h. In London ein Hotelzimmer zu finden, ist um diese Jahreszeit schwierig.

3N Saying the same thing differently

Ersetzen Sie die schräggedruckten Satzteile durch Formulierungen, die etwa dasselbe bedeuten.

a. This is not the *right* model.
b. I *returned* the damaged recorder to them.
c. They've *placed an order for* 250 Auto Deluxe toasters.
d. She *is very fond of* Stephen.
e. Malta is *a favourite* with British holidaymakers.
f. Malta's institutions and everyday life *resemble* England's *in many ways.*
g. The courier *told* them about their rooms, about sporting and recreation facilities, entertainment, *and so on.*
h. There's dancing *nightly* from 9.45 p.m. to 2.45 a.m.
i. *What* did you *do with yourselves all* day?
j. We're *thoroughly enjoying ourselves.*
k. They've just *returned* from Malta.

"Chief, I have good news and bad news. The bad news couldn't be worse and the good news couldn't be better. I also have some in-between news that couldn't be more so-so."

30 Ausdrücke mit Präpositionen

Prägen Sie sich die folgenden Ausdrücke mit Präpositionen gut ein.

about
about 10 minutes
ungefähr / etwa 10 Minuten
what do you like **about** Malta?
was gefällt dir an Malta?

at
arrive **at** the hotel
am / im Hotel ankommen
at night *am Abend*

beside
the table **beside** me
der Tisch neben mir

by
by the side of the swimming pool
am Rande des Schwimmbeckens

"The Hilton wasn't bad, but there's nothing like breakfast at home, is there really?"

from
different **from** *anders als*

in
he's interested **in** English
er interessiert sich für Englisch

in spite of
in spite of the rain
trotz des Regens

of
the republic **of** Malta
die Republik Malta
the island **of** Gozo *die Insel Gozo*
the Council **of** Europe *der Europarat*

on behalf of
on behalf of Maltese Tours
im Namen der Maltese Tours

throughout
throughout the hotel
im ganzen / überall im Hotel

to
explain it **to** me! *erkläre es mir!*
attractive **to** students
für Studierende attraktiv
welcome **to** Malta
willkommen in Malta

within
within walking distance *in Gehweite*

3P Dictation exercise

Hören Sie das Diktat vom Tonband und schreiben Sie dabei diejenigen Wörter nieder, die im folgenden Diktattext fehlen.

Malta became .... from the .... Kingdom in 1964.
There are about as many .... living in the Maltese .... as in Luxemburg, which has an .... over eight times as ....
The .... of the ...., Malta, is about the .... of the city of ....
Malta has a .... climate with hot summers and warm winters.
The Maltese .... are of .... race. The .... spoken by them are Maltese and English. The .... majoritiy of the population belong to the .... Catholic ....
There are three English and three Maltese .... newspapers and three .... newspapers.
Malta's main .... partners are ...., Italy, and West Germany. Tourism is .... more .... every year.

3Q Listening comprehension

Listen to the text on tape and complete the following table.

Rent for TV in hotel room	
Hotel shop's opening hours	
Foreign newspapers available after	
Foreign magazines available after	
Breakfast served from . . . to . . .	
Breakfast in bed: order from	
Sporting facilities	
Janet Stratford available: mornings	
evenings	

3R **Put in: about, around, beside, by, for, from, in, of, on, since, to, with.**

a. Malta is becoming a favourite ..... German holidaymakers.
b. It's about 180 miles ..... the North African coast.
c. A nice way of getting ..... the island is ..... horse-drawn cab.
d. Next time I go to Malta, I must look out ..... some nice hand-made glass objects.
e. Malta is pleasantly different ..... the tourist traps of Spain and Italy.
f. The Maltese islands are not only attractive ..... those who're interested ..... English.
g. Malta has been independent ..... Britain ..... 1964.
h. Stephen spent the morning sitting ..... the side ..... the swimming pool ..... a book ..... his hands and a cool drink ..... the table ..... him.
i. The courier welcomed us ..... the Malta Hilton and told us ..... the hotel's facilities.

"It was a great flight, they flew us from McDonald's to McDonald's in six hours forty-five minutes."

4I To-Infinitiv nach Verb + Objekt (→ GIV25, 19F)

Change the sentences as in the examples.

We'll arrange accommodation. (Would you like us . . .) Would you like us to arrange accommodation?
We'll prevent tragedies like this in future. (Please help us . . .) Please help us (to) prevent tragedies like this in future.

a. He'll stay in bed for the next few days. (The doctor wants him . . .)
b. Neighbours everywhere keep an eye on old people living alone. (We're appealing to neighbours . . .)
c. We're enjoying ourselves. (Do you expect us . . .)
d. She fetches Billy from school every day. (Can't we get her . . .)
e. They've sent us their latest catalogue. (I asked them . . .)
f. He phoned the emergency medical service. (I told him . . .)
g. The police believed that Mr Cole had been dead for five months. (What led the police . . .)
h. She wrote to a newspaper about her experience. (What made her . . .)

4J To-Infinitiv in relativsatzähnlicher Funktion (→ GIII21)

Make as many meaningful sentences as you can.

English is not an easy language For those interested in souvenirs, gold and silver objects are the things If there's no hotel, we must find some other place Immigrants have difficulty finding a decent place My husband is not an easy man On the promenade at the seaside you always have something She's an interesting person Some old people don't have enough money That was a silly thing There are many historical sights This company has an interesting job This is a good song What are suitable souvenirs	to bring home from Malta. to do. to learn. to live. to live on. to live with. to look at. to look out for. to offer. to see. to sing. to sleep. to talk to.

4K **Modale Hilfsverben**

He She They	should(n't) can't could(n't) may might must	have	phoned the emergency service. seen the film. read the book. stopped there. fetched the man's wife. entered the flat.

Translate as in the above examples.

a. Sie hätten den ärztlichen Notdienst anrufen sollen. (*should*)
b. Das hätte nicht passieren dürfen. (*shouldn't*)
c. Das ist etwas, was du nicht hättest auslassen dürfen. (*shouldn't*)
d. Der Milchmann kann die Flaschen nicht in den Kühlschrank gestellt haben. (*can't*)
e. Du hättest bei uns wohnen können. (*could*)
f. Wir hätten den Acht-Uhr-Zug von St Pancras nehmen können. (*could*)
g. Sie hätte das Fenster nicht allein öffnen können. (*couldn't*)
h. Er kann im Büro gewartet haben. (*may*)
i. Ein Urlaub in Malta wäre vielleicht ganz anders gewesen. (*might*)
j. Die Situation hätte gefährlich werden können. (*might*)
k. Ihr müßt den alten Mann gesehen haben. (*must*)

4L **Dictation exercise**

.... of people .... him, but nobody .... to help the old man who was sitting on the ground .... against a wall in the High Street at about 7 ....

.... white and trembling, he was .... unable to help himself. Had he .... a .... attack?

There were some .... across the road .... a shop that was still open.
They must have .... the old man, but they .... take any notice.
At last, the old man was .... by a woman .... a .... and a small dog. She .... to help him to his ...., but he was much too ....
So she left him .... on the ground and went and .... the .... medical service.

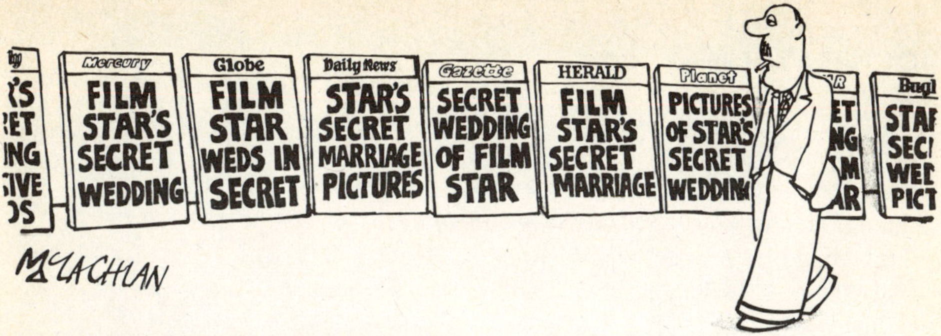

4M **Saying the same thing differently**

Ersetzen Sie die schräggedruckten Satzteile durch Formulierungen, die etwa dasselbe bedeuten.

a. I met him in the High Street *not so long* ago.
b. I managed to find out *his address.*
c. He *was too weak* to stand up.
d. He *was obviously a very sick man.*
e. I *phoned* the emergency medical service.
f. *He was seen by* dozens of people.
g. There were some *youths across* the road.
h. *I was told* that he died a week later.
i. We're *appealing to* neighbours to keep an eye on old people living alone.
j. She *doesn't have enough money to live on.*
k. She *has no contact with* other elderly people.
l. The doctor *visits* her regularly.
m. *He may have died* five months ago.

4N **Complete the following sentences to show that you understand the "new" words contained in them.**

a. The *weekly* rent is £20 – that is, they pay £20 a . . . . . b. An *icy* road is one with . . . . . on it. c. If a room is in complete *darkness,* that means that it is completely . . . . . d. His *weakness* was so great that he could not stand up. He was too . . . . . to stand up. e. A man's *childhood* is the time when he was a . . . . . f. There's a close *friendship* between the two women, that is they're close . . . . . g. An *armchair* is particularly comfortable because it is a . . . . . with arms. h. Something that causes you great *pain* is very . . . . . i. If someone has lost his *belief* in God, that means that he no longer . . . . . that there is a God. j. What is the *height* of Mount Everest? Mount Everest is 29,028 feet . . . . . k. The *length* of the lake is 24 miles, the maximum *width* is 5 miles, and the greatest *depth* is 623 feet. In other words, the lake is 24 miles . . . . . , 5 miles . . . . . , and 623 feet . . . . .

How are you feeling? *Wie fühlen Sie sich (denn so)?*
Fine, thanks. *Danke, gut / ausgezeichnet.*
Oh, not too / very well, I'm afraid. *Oh, leider nicht so sehr gut.*
I'm not feeling well. *Ich fühle mich nicht wohl.*
I'm feeling ill. *Ich fühle mich krank.*
I haven't been feeling at all well lately. *Ich fühle mich in letzter Zeit gar nicht gut / wohl.*
Is anything wrong? You don't look very well. *Fehlt Ihnen etwas? Sie sehen gar nicht gut aus.*
I've got a headache. *Ich habe Kopfschmerzen.*

The boy seems to have caught a cold. *Der Junge scheint sich erkältet zu haben.*
Have you taken his temperature? *Hast du seine Temperatur gemessen?*
He's running a temperature. / He's got a temperature. *Er hat Temperatur / Fieber.*
He's probably picked up some infection. *Er hat sich wahrscheinlich irgendwo angesteckt.*
He should go straight to bed. *Er sollte direkt ins Bett gehen.*

I think you ought to see a doctor. *Ich glaube, Sie sollten einen Arzt aufsuchen.*
You'd better see a doctor. *Es wäre besser, Sie gehen zum Arzt.*
Can you get me a doctor? *Können Sie mir einen Arzt holen?*
Please phone for the doctor. *Rufen Sie bitte den Arzt an, er möchte kommen.*
Please get me a doctor quickly. *Holen Sie mir bitte schnell einen Arzt.*
My appointment at the doctor's is at / for 11 o'clock. *Ich bin um / für 11 Uhr beim Arzt angemeldet.*
Dr Smith will see you after lunch. *Herr Dr. Smith kommt nach dem Mittagessen zu Ihnen / Sie können nach dem Mittagessen (zu Herrn Dr. Smith) kommen.*

What's wrong (then)? *Was fehlt Ihnen (denn)?*
What's the trouble / matter (then)? *Was für Beschwerden haben Sie (denn)?*
I often have headaches. *Ich habe oft Kopfschmerzen.*
I suffer from sleeplessness. *Ich leide unter Schlaflosigkeit.*
Do you feel any pain? *Haben Sie irgendwelche Schmerzen?*
I've got a pain in my back. *Ich habe Schmerzen im Rücken.*
I've got pains in my side. *Ich habe Schmerzen in der Seite.*

Where does it hurt? / Where's the pain? *Wo tut es weh? / Wo sind die Schmerzen?*
My arm / leg hurts. *Mir tut der Arm / das Bein weh.*
It hurts me here. *Hier tut es mir weh.*
How long have you had this pain? *Wie lange haben Sie diese Schmerzen schon?*
How long have you been feeling like this? *Wie lange geht es Ihnen schon so?*

Are you feeling any better? *Geht es Ihnen besser?*
I'm feeling worse / much better. *Es geht mir schlechter / viel besser.*
I'm feeling sick / depressed. *Ich fühle mich elend / niedergeschlagen.*
You'll have to take things easy for a while. *Sie werden sich eine Zeitlang schonen müssen.*
You'd better stay in bed for a day or two. *Sie bleiben besser ein paar Tage im Bett.*
I want you to stay in bed for the next few days. *Ich möchte, daß Sie die nächsten Tage im Bett bleiben.*
I hope you get better soon. / I hope you'll soon be better. *Gute Besserung!*
I hope you will soon get well again. *Hoffentlich sind Sie bald wieder gesund.*

"Excuse me asking, but where did you study acupuncture?"

"I'm here against medical advice, of course."

4P Ausdrücke mit Präpositionen

Prägen Sie sich die folgenden Ausdrücke mit Präpositionen gut ein.

across
the shop **across** the road *der Laden auf der anderen Straßenseite*

after
look **after** someone
sich um jemanden kümmern

against
lean **against** a wall
sich gegen / an eine Mauer lehnen

at
at the side of the road
am Straßenrand
at the doctor's *beim Arzt*

between
between us we managed . . .
gemeinsam schafften wir es . . .

for
she cried **for** help
sie rief um Hilfe

from
suffer **from** sleeplessness
unter Schlaflosigkeit leiden

in
in the street
auf der Straße

into
he went **into** hospital
er kam ins Krankenhaus

of
fear **of** illness
Angst vor Krankheit

on
live **on** £40 a week
von £40 in der Woche leben
be dependent **on** other people
von anderen Menschen abhängig sein
on a cold winter night
in einer kalten Winternacht / an einem kalten Winterabend

through
look **through** the window
durch das Fenster sehen

51 **Stellung des Adverbs** (→ GIII50, GIV12)

Vor dem Hauptverb:

> We **always** have a spare bed for you. *wir haben immer . . .*
> What do you **personally** think of this form of travel? *was halten Sie persönlich von . . .?*

Nach dem Hauptverb bzw. nach Hauptverb + Objekt:

> He comes here **regularly**. *er kommt regelmäßig hierher*
> He questioned her **thoroughly**. *er verhörte sie gründlich*

Put in the adverbs given in brackets.

a. He's picked up some sort of infection. (probably)
b. She sings. (beautifully)
c. Please get me a doctor. (quickly)
d. Malta is becoming a favourite with German holidaymakers. (rapidly)
e. My travel agent prepared everything. (carefully)
f. The policeman reported her. (obviously)
g. I know them. (very well)
h. If it was love at first sight, he didn't show it. (certainly)
i. You don't know what perfect love is till you've been married a quarter of a century. (really)
j. He did the whole job. (carelessly)
k. I go by taxi. (often / sometimes / never)
l. What do you like about Malta? (especially)
m. Who believes in love at first sight? (still)
n. He was sitting in an armchair. (comfortably)
o. "I've won the first prize," she cried. (happily) – She told him that she'd won the first prize. (happily)
p. The dog barks when a stranger comes up to the house. (always, loudly)

You don't know what perfect love is till you've been married a quarter of a century.

5J **Infinitive or (preposition plus) -ing form? Please complete.**

"Would you mind (tell) me what happened on 21st August?"
"Well, I found this old man lying on the pavement. I tried (lift) him up, but I couldn't. There were some other people in the street, I remember (see) them. They seemed (be) very busy – busy (talk). They saw us, but they didn't offer (help). And this is claimed (be) a Christian country! Anyway, I fetched the man's wife and then helped her (carry) him home. It took us about half an hour (get) him there. I promised (get) a doctor, but there wasn't any chance (phone) one until I got home."

5K **Change these sentences as in the example.**

He has been dead for five months. (When the old man's body was found . . .) When the old man's body was found, he had been dead for five months.

a. The letters have been lying there for five months. (When they were found . . .)
b. Mr Cole has always been very independent. (Neighbours said . . .)
c. She's only just arrived. (When I met her in the hotel lobby . . .)
d. Malta has been independent for ten years. (By 1974 . . .)
e. They've been living together for five years. (By the time he was forty . . .)

5L **Infinitiv nach Verb + Objekt** (→ 4I)

I **want you to stay** in bed for the next few days.
ich möchte, daß Sie . . . bleiben

Would you **like us to arrange** accommodation?
hätten Sie gern, daß wir . . . besorgen?

Translate as in the above examples.
a. Ich möchte, daß du dir dieses Buch hier anschaust. b. Hättest du gern, daß wir unsere Flitterwochen in Malta verbringen? c. Er möchte, daß wir uns um den alten Herrn kümmern. d. Hätten Sie gern, daß ich Ihnen etwas über die Einrichtungen des Hotels erzähle? e. Ich hätte gern, daß du ein nettes Mädchen mit ähnlichen Interessen kennenlernst. f. Ich möchte, daß Sie die (!) Füße vom Tisch nehmen. g. Ich möchte, daß du jetzt, wo wir heiraten, zu arbeiten aufhörst. h. Ich hätte gern, daß wir warten, bis das Gerichtsverfahren vorbei ist.

5M **Will be (un)able to**

"Können" in der Zukunft wird häufig durch *will be able to* ausgedrückt (vgl. AB1 14K, GIII41):

They hope they **will be able to** buy a house in the suburbs in a few years' time.	*... daß sie ... werden kaufen können ...*
We **won't be able to** come.	*wir werden nicht kommen können*
He'**ll be unable to** give evidence.	*er wird nicht aussagen können*

Please translate, using *will be (un)able to.*

a. Wirst du zu Susans Hochzeit kommen können? b. Leider (*afraid*) werde ich nicht kommen können. c. Wenn wir nach Malta fahren, werden wir viel englisch sprechen können. d. Wenn wir unser ganzes Geld für (*on*) Getränke ausgeben, werden wir keine Souvenirs kaufen können. e. Wenn sie hier wohnt, werden ihre Enkelkinder sie fast jeden Tag besuchen können. f. Wird sie ihren Haushalt allein führen (*manage*) können? g. Ihre Verwandten werden sich nicht um sie kümmern können. h. Wir hoffen, daß wir Tragödien wie diese in Zukunft verhindern können.

5N **Saying the same thing differently**

Ersetzen Sie die schräggedruckten Satzteile durch Formulierungen, die etwa dasselbe bedeuten.

a. Please *remember* to bring it along.
b. What's his *occupation*?
c. That kind of attitude is *hard* to understand.
d. Who did she *get married to*?
e. She's a *telephonist.*
f. He asked *if he could take her out.*
g. I *had no idea* she was getting married.
h. He's *a good-looking fellow.*
i. *Have you got* their address?
j. He wrote that he *was unable to come.*

They're both good-looking fellows.

5O **Ausdrücke mit Präpositionen**

Prägen Sie sich die folgenden Ausdrücke mit Präpositionen gut ein.

at	**in**
at St Giles Church *in der St.-Giles-Kirche*	**in** a public place *an einem öffentlichen Ort*
were you **at** the wedding? *waren Sie auf der Hochzeit?*	give evidence **in** court *vor Gericht aussagen*
love **at** first sight *Liebe auf den ersten Blick*	believe **in** something *an etwas glauben*

on	**to**
comment **on** something *sich zu etwas äußern*	she's married **to** a policeman *sie ist mit einem Polizisten verheiratet*
win **on** the pools *im Toto gewinnen*	in reply **to** the invitation *in Beantwortung der Einladung*

5P **Dictation exercise**

Hören Sie das Diktat vom Tonband und schreiben Sie dabei diejenigen Wörter nieder, die im folgenden Diktattext fehlen.

.... the way my .... Susan Williams met her ...., Michael! He was the .... who .... her when she had that .... car accident last year. He was very .... to her because she was so .... and ...., but he also questioned her ...., and when he .... that the accident was her ...., he booked her for .... driving. .... he gave .... against her in ....

For Michael it had .... love at first ...., but he didn't show it. It wasn't .... the .... case was over that he .... her and .... her out. After .... first .... dates they .... they were going to .... together, and last .... they got married – .... a year to the day since the accident that .... together.

6J -ing-Konstruktion in relativsatzähnlicher Funktion (→ GIII36)

Put in suitable verbs in the -ing form.

a. On coming home from work she found a stranger . . . . . in her living room.
b. The person . . . . . me to my seat in the theatre told me that the play was no good and that the gardener was the murderer.
c. The body was discovered by a neighbour . . . . . through the window of the flat.
d. When police entered the flat, they found letters and papers up to five months old . . . . . behind the front door.
e. Councillor Morris appealed to neighbours everywhere to keep an eye on old people . . . . . alone.
f. The draughtsmen . . . . . for our company are all well paid.
g. The lady . . . . . the phone had a "voice with a smile".
h. The cars and lorries . . . . . past our house make a lot of noise.
i. The policeman . . . . . her about the accident was very polite.
j. Most of the students . . . . . our courses are from Germany.

6K Partizip Perfekt in relativsatzähnlicher Funktion (→ LE1 30F, GIII38)

They were told that the room *booked* by them had been given to someone else.

Please complete as in the example.

a. Are there many young couples like the Swedish one . . . . . in the letter?
b. Use the information . . . . . in the table on the right.
c. Do you think the popularity of a country has something to do with the language . . . . . there?
d. Most housewives buy the products . . . . . in the TV commercials.
e. Most of the things . . . . . by the soothsayer came true.
f. The entertainment . . . . . at this hotel includes party games and dancing.
g. Most of the guests . . . . . to the wedding were colleagues of the bride.
h. The shoes . . . . . by this company are among the best on the market.
i. We are sorry that we are unable to give the information . . . . . by Mr Blake.
j. The wages . . . . . by this company are all above average.

6L Make two sentences into one as in the example.

I spent the first five years of my life in London. Then I started my primary education at King Edward's School, Dover.
After spending the first five years of my life in London, I started my primary education at King Edward's School, Dover.

a. I finished primary school at the age of eleven. Then I attended St John's Grammar School, Croydon, up to the age of eighteen.
b. He studied at Oxford. Then he became a clerk in the Patent Office.
c. I ate a light supper. Then I went up to my room.
d. He pottered about in the garden for about two hours. Then he joined his wife for tea.
e. She phoned the emergency medical service. Then she went and fetched the man's wife.
f. They got married at St Giles Church, West Bridgford. Then they went to Malta for a two-week honeymoon.
g. Carter served in the U.S. Navy for six years. Then he returned to civilian life to become a peanut farmer and warehouseman.
h. The policeman questioned her thoroughly. Then he reported her because the crash was her fault.
i. Elaine finished her meal. Then she discovered that she had no money on her.

6M Need not

Positiv:

The answers given by you **must** / **should** all be true.
müssen / sollten alle stimmen

Negativ:

The answers given by you **need not** / **needn't** all be true.
brauchen nicht alle zu stimmen

Make the following sentences negative by using need not / needn't. ⚭

a. The crash must be reported.
b. You should phone a doctor.
c. This form here must be filled in.
d. We should have a meeting before the holidays.
e. You must bring your leaving certificate with you.
f. We should tell them that we're coming.

"We needn't be absolutely punctual, need we?"

6N **Must – needn't**

Must we send them flowers or something? No, we / you needn't.

Give answers as in the example. ⚭

a. Must we go to the meeting?
b. Must we arrange accommodation for him?
c. Must I be absolutely punctual?
d. Must it be an intensive course?
e. Must the underwear and pyjamas be ironed?
f. Must the room be air-conditioned?
g. Must these questions be answered too?

6O **Is it necessary for . . . to . . .?**

Change the sentences in 6N as in the following example. ⚭

Must we send them flowers or something? – No, we needn't. Is it necessary for us to send them flowers or something? – No, it isn't.

6P **Use and non-use of a(n). Please translate.**

a. Er ist amerikanischer Staatsbürger. b. Der Verfasser dieses Buches, Peter Underwood, ist Präsident des Ghost Club. c. Von 1962 bis 1966 war Carter Mitglied des Senats von Georgia. d. Von 1971 bis 1974 war er Gouverneur von Georgia. e. Als Busfahrer verdient man ungefähr 80 Pfund in der Woche. f. Ich habe Kopfschmerzen. g. Der Junge hat Temperatur. h. Ich habe Schmerzen im Rücken. i. Es ist schade, daß wir unseren Urlaub nicht in Malta verbringen können. j. Was für eine Überraschung! k. Was für ein(e Art von) Bier trinkt man hier?

6Q **Position of a(n). Please translate.**

a. Das ist ein ziemlicher Unterschied. b. Das ist ein ziemlich weiter Weg. c. Was für ein herrlicher Baum das (doch) ist! d. Es kostete (*take*) uns ungefähr eine halbe Stunde. e. Warum ist Malta so ein attraktiver Ort? f. So mancher Liberaler ist ein Konservativer geworden.

6R **Dictation exercise**

Hören Sie das Diktat vom Tonband und schreiben Sie dabei diejenigen Wörter nieder, die im folgenden Diktattext fehlen.

Georgia (so named after the English king George II) was .... in 1733, and in .... became the .... state of the United States.
About 8 .... of Georgia's population work in .... Peanuts, cotton, maize, and .... are the .... agricultural products.
The .... of Georgia is mild, with temperatures between an .... winter minimum of 5 .... and an .... summer maximum of 33 ....
Georgia's ...., Atlanta, a .... modern city with a population of about half a million, ... its first black .... in 1973.
Atlanta has .... institutions of .... education, ... them the Georgia Institute of Technology, which was founded in ....
One of the .... most popular products, Coca-Cola, comes from Atlanta. The .... drink was first mixed there by Dr S. Pemberton in .... Today the Coca-Cola Company sells over .... million .... a day in more .... 130 ....

Skyline of Atlanta, Georgia, the "Coca-Cola city". The state capital has a population of 500,000, half of them black. Average family income here ranges from more than $30,000 a year in the richest areas to less than $2,000 in the poorest slums.

6S Listening comprehension

Listen to the texts on tape and choose the right answer.

a. You can see Mrs Biggs
   1 after a meeting that ends between 10.30 and 11 o'clock.
   2 at 10.45.
   3 between 8.30 and about 11 o'clock.
   4 from 10.30 to 11 o'clock.

b. You have booked for 2 weeks, so you will
   1 be staying at the Hilton at first but it will cost you more money.
   2 give Maltese Tours the bill for the Sea View Hotel.
   3 have to stay at the Sea View Hotel for 3 days.
   4 stay for 3 days at the Hilton Hotel and 11 days at the Sea View Hotel.

c. The man wants you to
   1 have a look at his wife's leg.
   2 help him lift his wife up.
   3 phone the doctor.
   4 wait with his wife.

d. Your friend wants you to
   1 bring some close friends to his party.
   2 come to his wedding on the 7th.
   3 help him celebrate his wedding anniversary on the 7th.
   4 visit him next weekend.

e. You can't walk with your leg, so you go
   1 straight to the doctor's.
   2 straight to the hospital.
   3 to the doctor's first and then to the hospital.
   4 to the hospital first and then to the doctor's.

"Do try to make it this evening. We so seldom see ordinary people."
(seldom = selten)

7H Aktiv – Passiv: Vergangenheitsform

Aktiv:	Dozens of people saw him. *Dutzende von Leuten sahen ihn*
Passiv:	He was seen by dozens of people. *er wurde von Dutzenden von Leuten gesehen*

Change the following sentences into the passive as in the example.

a. A neighbour discovered the body.
b. A gang of youths mugged him in a New York subway station.
c. Joern Utzon designed the Sydney Opera House.
d. Her mother answered the phone.
e. A reporter from the *Evening Herald* interviewed her.
f. Mrs Harris heard the girl's screams.
g. Mark Twain wrote this letter.
h. An Alsatian bit the little girl.

7I Aktiv – Passiv: modale Hilfsverben

Aktiv:	You shouldn't sack him. *Sie sollten ihn nicht entlassen*
Passiv:	He shouldn't be sacked. *er sollte nicht entlassen werden*
Aktiv:	Must we really change the plans? *müssen wir die Pläne wirklich ändern?*
Passiv:	Must the plans really be changed? *müssen die Pläne wirklich geändert werden?*

Change the following sentences into the passive as in the example.

a. You shouldn't allow them to watch television.
b. You must keep it spotlessly clean.
c. We can't turn it on till June the tenth.
d. We ought to keep the windows closed.
e. We can't sell it at this price.
f. Can you translate these letters?
g. Can't you give the room to someone else?
h. Won't they turn on the air conditioning?
i. Shouldn't someone meet him at the airport?
j. What time must we pick up the tickets?

"If he says it can't be done, sack him and g[…] a man who doesn't say it can't be done."

7J **Passiv. – Please translate.**

a. Carter wurde 1976 gewählt. b. Das Sydney Opera House wurde 1973 eröffnet. c. Die Kosten werden auf 7 Millionen Dollar geschätzt. d. Die Abkürzung *Ms* wird heutzutage zunehmend gebraucht. e. Das Zimmer ist jemand anders gegeben worden. f. Der Hund war von seinem Herrn grausam behandelt worden. g. Die Fenster müssen geschlossen gehalten werden. h. Ich glaube nicht, daß er wiedergewählt (werden) wird.

7K **Gebrauch des Perfekts** (→ AB1 GIII14)

a. They **have been married** (for) over ten years. *sie* sind *jetzt über zehn Jahre / seit über zehn Jahren* verheiratet
b. I **haven't been feeling** at all well lately. *ich* fühle mich *in der letzten Zeit gar nicht gut*
c. How long **have you had** this pain in the leg? *wie lange* haben Sie schon *diese Schmerzen im Bein?*

Das Perfekt steht im Englischen nicht nur für Handlungen, die bereits stattgefunden haben (*I have taken his temperature*), sondern anders als im Deutschen auch für Handlungen und Zustände, die in der Vergangenheit begonnen haben und in der Gegenwart noch andauern (oben a–c).

Make sentences as in the examples.

the Browns / be / married / five years The Browns have been married for five years now.
Mr Stewart / be / away from the office / the beginning of the week Mr Stewart has been away from the office since the beginning of the week.
how long / you / have / this pain in the leg How long have you had this pain in the leg?

a. the President / be / in office / almost a year b. my father / be / in hospital / exactly ten days c. the house / be / unoccupied / Mrs Nelson died d. we / have / our swimming pool / two years e. I / have / this account / I moved here three years ago f. I / want / to visit Glasgow / you wrote to me in January g. how long / you / live / at this address h. how many years / you / be / employed at Interoil

7L Gebrauch des Perfekts

Make sentences as in the examples.

Mr Erdem / work / on the assembly line / six months Mr Erdem has been working on the assembly line for six months now.
Mrs Thompson / live / alone / her husband died Mrs Thompson has been living alone since her husband died.
how long / you / live / at your present address How long have you been living at your present address?

a. the Hendersons / live / in Harlington / two years
b. these old books / lie / here / at least three months
c. we / learn / English / over two years
d. the boy / run / a temperature / he came back from the excursion
e. I / look / out for a suitable souvenir / I arrived
f. she / suffer / from sleeplessness / she had that accident last May
g. Susan and Michael / dance / together / they came
h. my wife / play / tennis / the club was founded about three years ago
i. how long / you / attend / this school
j. how long / Dr Brown / treat / you
k. how long / you / feel / like this

7M Gebrauch des Perfekts

Please translate.

a. Wir sind jetzt seit einem Vierteljahrhundert verheiratet. b. Wie lange haben Sie diese Schmerzen schon? c. Wie lange ist Ihr Vater schon im Krankenhaus? d. Wie lange seht ihr schon fern, Kinder? e. Ich fühle mich in letzter Zeit gar nicht gut. f. Er wohnt jetzt seit drei Jahren hier. g. Ich spiele Fußball seit meinem zehnten Lebensjahr ("seit ich zehn war"). h. Ich lerne jetzt seit drei Jahren Englisch.

"We've been coming here for our picnics for years."

7N **Dictation exercise** ○○

Hören Sie das Diktat vom Tonband und schreiben Sie dabei diejenigen Wörter nieder, die im folgenden Diktattext fehlen.

Australia is over .... times the .... of West Germany but has less .... a .... of West Germany's population.
.... per cent of Australia's population live in cities; .... per cent in and .... Sydney and Melbourne alone.
Australia's national income per person is .... the same as West Germany's; it is much higher .... Austria's but lower .... Switzerland's.
Australia's .... fall at .... times of the .... from Central Europe's: spring is from September to December, summer from December to ...., autumn (['ɔːtəm] = *Herbst*) from .... to June, and winter from June to September.

View of Central Sydney from the north shore of Port Jackson, Sydney's natural harbour. In the foreground is Sydney Harbour Bridge, one of the largest steel-arch bridges in the world.

70 Complete the text by putting in the following words.

along, asked, between, could, couldn't, country, deathly, do, don't, fetched, found, got, group, happened, help, helped, home, hope, just, leaning, left, lived, motorists, only, open, people, phoned, rest, see, sitting, tell, then, took, trembling, weak, why, will, write

Mrs Wilson (→ 4A) arrives . . . . . on the evening when she . . . . . the old man lying in the street. She tells her husband what has . . . . .

Mr W Who have you just . . . . . ?

Mrs W The emergency medical service.

Mr W The emergency medical service! . . . . . ?

Mrs W Well, you see, on my way home I . . . . . an old man lying in the road – well, not actually lying in the road, he was . . . . . on the ground, against a wall, ... against a wall, you see. In the High Street it was, outside Woolworth's.

Mr W Oh dear. Accident?

Mrs W No, he was ill, very ill. He was all . . . . . white and . . . . . all over.

Mr W What did you . . . . . then?

Mrs W Well, he was very . . . . . , and I'm not very strong of course, so I couldn't . . . . . him up, up on to his feet. And . . . . . I had my shopping basket and the dog with me, too.

Mr W Well, you could have put them down, ... you?

Mrs W Hm, yes, I suppose I . . . . . I didn't think. I was so excited. Well, anyway, I couldn't . . . . . him up so I . . . . . him what his name was and where he . . . . . Well, he managed to . . . . . me that, so I . . . . . him there where he was, ... on the ground, and went and . . . . . his wife. I was lucky; they . . . . . lived about three hundred yards away.

Mr W Yes, that was lucky. And what . . . . . ?

Mrs W Well, I . . . . . his wife and . . . . . us we managed to get him . . . . . to his home. It . . . . . us nearly half an hour.

Mr W Phew! Half an hour for three hundred yards?

Mrs W Yes, he was so heavy, you . . . . . Well, anyway, we . . . . . him home and then I came home, and, well, you know the . . . . . , I've . . . . . rung the emergency medical service. I . . . . . he's going to be all right.

Mr W Yes. – Didn't anybody help you carry the old man . . . . . ?

Mrs W Well yes – no they didn't. I mean, that's the point. Dozens of . . . . . saw us – pedestrians and . . . . . There was a shop that was still . . . . . , you . . . . . , and quite a lot of people stopped there, and there was a . . . . . of youths outside, too.

Mr W But nobody . . . . . you.

Mrs W Nobody.

Mr W And we are a Christian . . . . . I mean, we always say we are, ... we? Why don't you . . . . . to the paper about this?

Mrs W Hm, I think I . . . . .

7P **Do you know the right answer?**

a. Australia was discovered at the beginning of the (1) 15th century.
(2) 16th
(3) 17th

b. The Australian head of state is the (1) British king (= *König*) or queen.
(2) President.
(3) Prime Minister.

c. Nearly (1) 10 per cent of Australia's population were not born in Australia.
(2) 25
(3) 40

d. Australians drink (1) about as much beer as Germans do.
(2) much less beer than
(3) much more beer than

e. The air distance between Sydney and Berlin is about (1) 13,100 kilometres.
(2) 16,100
(3) 19,100

f. "Rattle your dags!" is Australian for (1) "Cheers!"
(2) "Get a move on!"
(3) "Put your hands up!"

g. "Have a Captain Cook" is Australian for (1) "have a drink".
(2) "have a holiday".
(3) "have a look".

8G Zum Gebrauch der Artikel a(n) und the

Die Artikel werden im Englischen mitunter anders gebraucht als im Deutschen. Beispiele:

Englisch: mit Artikel – Deutsch: ohne Artikel

I've got **a headache**. *ich habe Kopfschmerzen*
My father was **an architect**. *mein Vater war Architekt*

Englisch: ohne Artikel – Deutsch: mit Artikel

It was love at **first sight**. *es war Liebe auf den ersten Blick*
How did you spend **Christmas Day**?
wie habt ihr den ersten Weihnachtstag verbracht?

Put in a(n) or the where necessary.

a. It's . . . . . pity that our shop isn't in . . . . . High Street.
b. The girl that was bitten by the dog had to be taken to . . . . . hospital.
c. The ambulance took her to . . . . . big hospital in . . . . . Mortimer Street.
d. I finished . . . . . primary school at . . . . . age of ten.
e. As . . . . . toolmaker he worked about 45 hours . . . . . week.
f. When I visited him . . . . . other day, he said he had . . . . . bad pain in his back.
g. The boy has . . . . . temperature. He's probably caught . . . . . cold.
h. My father gets up at . . . . . sunrise and goes to . . . . . bed at . . . . . midnight.
i. He usually travels to . . . . . work by . . . . . bus, but sometimes he takes . . . . . underground.
j. 16 per cent of Austria's population work in . . . . . agriculture.
k. . . . . . life is hard for us at . . . . . moment. . . . . . things can only get better.
l. Being . . . . . mother of four myself, I take . . . . . keen interest in my children's progress.
m. This book shows . . . . . American life as it really is.
n. After being promoted to . . . . . rank of . . . . . lieutenant in 1950, Carter returned to . . . . . civilian life in 1953 to become . . . . . peanut farmer and . . . . . warehouseman.
o. Carter was . . . . . member of . . . . . Georgia Senate from 1962–66, and . . . . . Governor of Georgia from 1971–74.

8H **Indirekte Rede** (→ 5H, GIV20)

Change the following sentences as in the examples.

"Parents *are* becoming increasingly critical of 'progressive' textbooks." (He said . . .) He said that parents *were* becoming increasingly critical of "progressive" textbooks.
"*My* religious feelings *are* offended when a textbook *treats* Biblical stories as myths." (A youngster complained . . .) A youngster complained that *his* religious feelings *were* offended when a textbook *treated* Biblical stories as myths.

a. "The pictures are unsuitable for ten-year-olds." (Experts pointed out . . .)
b. "The textbooks show people as they really are." (The teachers responsible argued . . .)
c. "We don't want our children to read texts reflecting moral and political attitudes quite different from our own." (Parents said . . .)
d. "They may help children in their own lives." (Teachers defended the use of such reading materials by saying . . .)
e. "The textbooks used in my son's school contain a lot of violence, sex scenes, and gutter language." (An angry mother complained . . .)
f. "The Bible also contains a lot of violence, sex, and strong language." (A teacher reacted by saying . . .)

8I **Indirekte Rede** (→ 5H, GIV20)

Change the following sentences as in the examples here and in 8H.

"Why *didn't you give* it to someone else?" (They asked her . . .) They asked her why *she hadn't given* it to someone else.
"*Will you be able* to give me a bed for the night of Wednesday, 19th?" (I was wondering . . .) I was wondering if / whether *you would be able* to give me a bed for the night of Wednesday, 19th.

a. "Why didn't you write earlier?" (He asked her . . .) b. "Who won?" (He wondered . . .) c. "How long did it take to build the bridge?" (They wanted to know . . .) d. "When is Susan getting married?" (They had no idea . . .) e. "What's your name?" (He asked her . . .) f. "Why do the windows have to be kept closed?" (She wondered . . .) g. "Will you be in London for the wedding?" (He asked me . . .) h. "Will you be able to meet me at the airport?" (She asked him . . .) i. "Will the foundations be strong enough to hold the roof?" (The engineers were asked . . .) j. "Is the play any good?" (She wanted to know . . .) k. "Do you like that sort of poetry?" (The teacher asked her . . .) l. "Did you fill in the questionnaire?" (She asked him . . .)

8J **Indirekte Rede**

Please translate.

a. Er sagte, sein Name sei Harris. b. Der Manager dachte, ich sei betrunken. c. Er fragte sie, ob er mit ihr ausgehen könne. d. Sie sagte mir, daß das (Theater-)Stück nicht gut sei und daß der Gärtner der Mörder sei. e. Der Autor fragte seinen Verleger, wie sich (denn) sein neuester Roman verkaufe. f. Sie schrieb, sie sei selbst Mutter von vier Kindern. g. Er erzählte mir, daß sein Vater sehr (*absolutely*) wütend gewesen sei. h. Die Lehrerin sagte uns, daß unsere Kinder nach einer sehr fortschrittlichen Methode unterrichtet würden.

8K **Ausdrücke mit Präpositionen**

about
what's this book **about**?
wovon handelt dieses Buch?

at
study **at** a university
an / auf einer Universität studieren
at the age of ten
im Alter von zehn Jahren
he gets up **at** sunrise
er steht bei Sonnenaufgang auf

by
by what name is he known?
unter welchem Namen ist er bekannt?
teach **by** a progressive method
nach einer fortschrittlichen Methode unterrichten

for
apply **for** a job *sich um einen Arbeitsplatz bewerben*
apply **for** a loan
ein Darlehen beantragen
an application **for** a loan
ein Antrag auf ein Darlehen
wait **for** someone *auf jem. warten*
what does he do **for** a living?
womit verdient er sich seinen Lebensunterhalt?
for fear of death *aus Angst vor d. Tode*

from
where does this word come **from**?
wo kommt dieses Wort her?
A is different **from** B
A ist anders als B

in

if you were **in** my place

wenn du an meiner Stelle wärest

the best car **in** the world

das beste Auto (auf) der Welt

take an interest **in** something

sich für etwas interessieren

of

it consists **of** three parts

es besteht aus drei Teilen

she's suspicious **of** him

sie ist ihm gegenüber mißtrauisch

what do you think **of** fairy tales?

was halten Sie von Märchen?

off

get **off** the bus *aus dem Bus aussteigen*

on

get **on** the bus *in den Bus einsteigen*

work **on** the assembly line

am Fließband arbeiten

spend money **on** something

Geld für etwas ausgeben

Georgia borders **on** the Atlantic

Georgia grenzt an den Atlantik

he was born **on** October 1, 1924

er wurde am 1. Oktober 1924 geboren

out of

take something **out of** context

etwas aus dem Zusammenhang reißen

"If you were in my place – what would you do?"

up to

up to now *bis jetzt*

up to the age of eleven

bis zum Alter von elf Jahren

with

I haven't got it **with** me

ich habe es nicht bei mir

he's popular **with** the masses

er ist bei den Massen beliebt

"I've been off sick – have teaching methods become more progressive again?"

8L Put in: at, by, for, from, in, nor, of, on, to, with.

a. Carter comes . . . . . Georgia. He was born . . . . . Plains . . . . . October 1, 1924.
Georgia lies north . . . . . Florida and borders . . . . . the Atlantic.
Carter got married . . . . . the age . . . . . twenty-two.
He studied . . . . . the Georgia Institute . . . . . Technology and the U.S. Naval Academy.
Carter became President because he was very popular . . . . . the masses.

b. When one asks parents what they think . . . . . their children's school textbooks, one finds that many people are critical . . . . . the texts contained . . . . . them. Our children are taught . . . . . the most progressive methods, but according . . . . . Mrs Watson, who works . . . . . the personnel department . . . . . a large company, an increasing number . . . . . youngsters applying . . . . . work are neither literate . . . . . numerate. As a result . . . . . this sort of experience, many people are becoming suspicious . . . . . "progressive" methods.

8M Dictation exercise

Sir,

Like many _____ parents of teenage children I am becoming _____ worried by the textbooks used in _____ schools. I find it _____ that there should be so many texts _____ violence, sex _____ or "gutter" language. Often _____ the reading material _____ moral and political _____ quite different from _____ of the _____ of parents.

The _____ defend these books by saying that they _____ better _____ parents what kind of texts are _____ for children, that the _____ textbooks are progressive and have been _____ by experts, that they _____ life as it _____ is, and that the _____ to be learnt from them can help the children in _____ own _____ . I _____ that times have _____ since my own school days and that the textbooks used _____ may not be _____ for _____ youngsters, but _____ it _____ if some of the texts used _____ seem to _____ the values the children are _____ at home?

Yours _____,

Susan Cole

9I To-Infinitiv, -ing-Form oder Präposition + -ing-Form?

Don't **forget** [to bring] the tickets along.	(*to* infinitive)
What did he do after he **finished** [studying] ?	(-*ing* form)
Instead [of going] on wild spending sprees, he invested his money wisely.	(preposition + -*ing* form)

Put in the correct forms of the verbs in brackets (to infinitive, -ing form or preposition + -ing form).

a. They decided (bring) in a law against the killing of dogs for their skins. b. It's my turn (buy) drinks now. c. It was a pleasure (serve) you, sir. d. Fancy (meet) you here, Jack! e. We were sorry (hear) that your flight was not very pleasant. f. Would you mind (tell) me how you managed (get) the money? g. I've arranged (meet) him during the second half of January. h. It used (be) a lot of fun (work) in the canteen. i. We look forward (see) you here on the 20th. j. He didn't take time off for fear (be) sacked. k. His friends couldn't help (wonder) how he had managed (spend) his pools win so quickly. l. We were delighted (hear) that you'll be over here on 19th January. m. On the way, we stopped (pay) a short visit to John Brown's farm near Lake Placid. n. I would be interested (know) what your parents think about it. o. This house has the advantage (be) fairly near the town centre. p. Would you go on (work) if you won £185,000 on the pools? q. He had promised (meet) her at the airport. r. Instead (phone) the emergency medical service right away, Mrs Wilson went and fetched the man's wife. s. I don't intend (drink) myself to death now that I get free beer. t. The future is something Dennis Bryan refuses (think) about. u. I'm not fond (spend) the day pottering about in the garden; I'm thinking (go) back to work. v. I was disturbed (find) so many texts containing violence, sex scenes or "gutter" language in the book.

9J -ing-Konstruktion als Subjekt (→ GIII29)

It isn't fun to live in a house like this one.
Living in a house like this one isn't fun.
in einem Haus wie diesem zu wohnen, ist kein Vergnügen

Change the following sentences as in the above example. ꝏ

a. It's great fun to shop in the crowded streets and markets. b. It's difficult to find a decent place to live. c. It's important to have people like The Samaritans. d. It was a particular pleasure for me to come to your home. e. Is it a crime to commit suicide? f. It doesn't satisfy you in the long run to potter about in the garden all day. g. It took them about half an hour to get him along to his home. h. It can be harmful for the eyes to watch too much television. i. It must be hard to be unable to manage one's own household. j. It'll cost you a lot of money to get a divorce.

9K **Adjektiv oder Adverb? Mit oder ohne -ly?** (→ GIV8)

Complete the sentences by putting in words from the following list.

easy / easily, expensive / expensively, generous / generously, good / well, hard / hardly, helpless / helplessly, possible / possibly, terrible / terribly, wise / wisely

a. Could you . . . . . drive me to the airport tomorrow morning?
b. Dennis Bryan won a fortune on the pools, but instead of investing his winnings . . . . ., he spent most of his money on a sports car, an . . . . . flat in Mayfair, and . . . . . presents for a night-club hostess.
c. Do you think it would be . . . . . to buy a car which is so . . . . . expensive?
d. The migrants have to struggle . . . . . to get by; they feel alone and . . . . .; they have . . . . . any friends in their new country.
e. You can . . . . . catch a cold if you work outside all day in this rain.
f. You know me . . . . . enough to say "no" without any fuss.
g. If he wasn't an animal lover, he wouldn't treat his dog so . . . . .

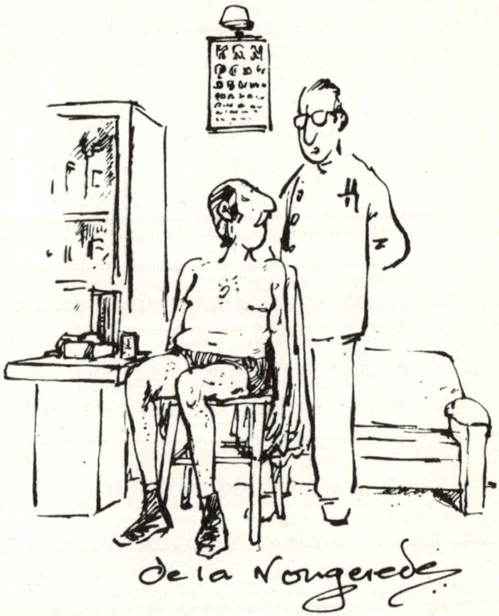

h. *"If you want to get . . . . . again, you'll have to take things . . . . . for a while."*

9L "Können"

Please translate, using the following words.

be able to, be unable to, can, could, may, might

a. Kann ich Ihnen behilflich sein?

b. Er kann die Maschine selber (*himself*) reparieren.

c. Wir können jetzt von den Zinsen leben.

d. Wie konnte sie mir das antun?

e. Er wollte hinausgehen, aber er konnte die Tür nicht öffnen.

f. Sie konnten nicht die Art von Arbeit finden, für die sie ausgebildet worden waren.

g. Er konnte die Maschine selber reparieren.

h. Werden Sie diesen Brief übersetzen können?

i. Ich fürchte, wir werden nicht kommen können.

j. Es kann sein, daß er noch zu Hause ist. ("Er kann noch zu Hause sein.")

k. Weißt du, wo er ist? – Nein, aber er könnte noch im Büro sein.

l. Seine Adresse kann sich geändert haben.

m. Er kann die Maschine nicht selber repariert haben.

9M Dictation exercise

Hören Sie das Diktat vom Tonband und schreiben Sie dabei diejenigen Wörter nieder, die im folgenden Diktattext fehlen.

When Jim Mitchell .... £170,000 on the .... two years ago, he didn't .... his ....

Most of his .... have been ...., and Jim, his wife Betty, and .... three children live .... the ....

The .... hasn't .... the family very much. Jim still drinks his $2^{1}/_{2}$ .... at the pub .... the corner .... a ...., and the Mitchells haven't .... on any spending .... or .... the .... bungalow.

Of ...., there are now things the Mitchells can do .... they couldn't do .... they .... the .... For ...., right after Jim .... the .... from .... Laura McDonald, he .... his wife on a three-and-a-..........-month .... the world, and this .... they are .... to spend four .... touring ....

9N **Ausdrücke mit Präpositionen**

about
think **about** the future
an die Zukunft denken
he doesn't remember much **about** it
er weiß nicht mehr viel davon

around
walk **around** Manchester
in Manchester umhergehen

as
as people we have not altered
als Menschen haben wir uns nicht verändert

at
he's a canteen attendant **at** Empire Machines *er ist Kantinenangestellter bei Empire Machines*
my mates **at** the factory
meine Kumpels in der Fabrik

by
he has downed his first glass of brandy **by** the time he gets out of bed
bevor er aufsteht, hat er schon sein erstes Glas Brandy getrunken

for
a cheque **for** £200
ein Scheck über £200

in
if you were **in** my position
wenn du an meiner Stelle wärest

of
think **of** something *an etwas denken*

off
they can live **off** the interest
sie können von den Zinsen leben

on
win money **on** the football pools
Geld im Fußballtoto gewinnen

round
a journey **round** the world
eine Reise um die Welt

till
he sleeps **till** noon
er schläft bis Mittag

to
they had never been **to** a night club before *sie waren noch nie in einem Nachtklub gewesen*
she took a fancy **to** him
sie fand Gefallen an ihm
he treated her **to** champagne
er spendierte ihr Champagner

"If you win a quarter of a million, can I have a bit more on the housekeeping?"

9O Listening comprehension

Listen to the text on tape and decide whether the following statements are True (T) or Not True (NT).

a. The boy says it is wrong to say people are not literate because they can't fill in forms easily.
b. The boy says some school leavers make wild generalizations when filling in forms.
c. The boy says some people need all their life to learn to spell correctly, but they do learn to eventually.
d. The boy says not being able to read and write well shouldn't make people second-class citizens.
e. The boy says some of the people in his class have decided to become bricklayers and dressmakers.
f. The boy says forms are often written in a special language ordinary people don't use.
g. The boy says bureaucrats and officials are the only people who find it easy to fill in forms.
h. The boy thinks people in Mrs Watson's generation could read and write better.
i. The boy says schoolchildren don't have enough time to learn to spell properly because there is so much else to learn.
j. The boy says English and the funny language used in forms are two languages that are difficult to spell.

9P Put in: about, around, as, at, for, in, of, off, on, round, through, to.

a. I'm not fond . . . . . pottering . . . . . in the garden and walking . . . . . Manchester all the time.
b. . . . . . the long run it's boring to have nothing to do.
c. . . . . . people we have not altered at all; we're still counting the pennies . . . . . habit.
d. If you win money . . . . . the football pools, you shouldn't spend it . . . . . night clubs and such things. A journey . . . . . the world is a much better idea, or you may invest the money so you can live . . . . . the interest.
e. . . . . . the day I got the cheque . . . . . £185,000, I treated all my mates . . . . . the factory . . . . . champagne.

10J Frageanhängsel ("nicht wahr?" – "oder (doch)?" – "was?")

(→ AB1 21K, LE1 24H, GIV35)

Bejahte Aussage – verneintes Frageanhängsel:

Bejaht		Verneint	
It's **He works**	a lot of work, here,	**isn't it?** **doesn't he?**	*es ist viel Arbeit, nicht wahr?* *er arbeitet hier, nicht wahr?*

Verneinte Aussage – bejahtes Frageanhängsel:

Verneint		Bejaht	
You don't **That's not**	know what we make, a bad idea,	**do you?** **is it?**	*sie wissen nicht, . . ., oder (doch)?* *das ist keine schlechte Idee, was?*

Add question tags (= Frageanhängsel) to the following sentences.

a. Miss Hopkiss is a customer of ours, ...
b. Parking isn't allowed here, ...
c. That's bad luck, ...
d. Her car wasn't towed away, ...
e. You were in town this morning, ...
f. It could just as well have been stolen, ...
g. You've got to pay six pounds, ...
h. You don't have any coins on you, ...
i. You saw it being towed away, ...
j. It doesn't matter, ...
k. He didn't pick up a ticket, ...
l. You want to know what's happened to your car, ...
m. You didn't park it in the middle of the road, ...

This meter is out of order, isn't it?
You don't have to put any money in, do you?

10K **Do, be, have und modale Hilfsverben als "Stellvertreter" eines längeren Ausdrucks** (→ GIII47)

We say we are a Christian country. **Are** we really (a Christian country)?
I suppose all the parking meters were taken. – No, for once they **weren't** (taken).
I wonder if young people nowadays like that kind of poetry. – I'm sure some of them **do** (= like that kind of poetry).

Complete the following sentences, using any of the following words: do(n't) / does(n't) / did(n't), have(n't) / had(n't), am / are / was(n't), can / couldn't, will / would, should(n't).

Did you pick up a parking ticket? – Yes, I did.
Have you got your driving licence on you? – No, I haven't.
My car was towed away, but hers wasn't.
They tried to tow it away, but they couldn't.

a. Have you put a coin in? – Yes, I . . . . .
b. Do you have any shopping to do? – No, I . . . . .
c. Should children be allowed to watch as much TV as they like? – No, they . . . . .
d. Had it been stolen? – No, it . . . . .
e. You must be pretty busy. – Yes, I . . . . .
f. Who knows where the car pound is? – I . . . . .
g. I wonder if he remembers my name. – I'm sure he . . . . .
h. You must come and see us soon. – Yes, I . . . . .
i. I thought it might have been towed away, but it . . . . .
j. I can't tell you where it was, but my wife . . . . .
k. She tried to open the door but . . . . .
l. At first I didn't like her, but now I . . . . .
m. We wanted to visit her in hospital, but the doctor said we . . . . .
n. I thought it wouldn't matter, but it . . . . .
o. All the other parking meters were taken, but this one . . . . .
p. The policeman said I'd parked it in the middle of the road, but I . . . . .
q. I paid twenty-six p for it, and so . . . . . my wife.
r. I'm going to give up smoking, and so . . . . . you.
s. The police said it was causing an obstruction, and it . . . . .
t. I didn't stay as long as they said I . . . . .
u. Buying that present for my wife took much longer than I thought it . . . . .

10L **Stellung des Objekts bei zusammengesetzten Verben**
(→ GIII48, 18H)

1. They've [towed] [away] **the red Ford Cortina that was parked on the corner**.
2. They've [towed] [away] **my car**, but not yours.
3. They've [towed] **my car** [away] .
4. They've [towed] **it** [away] .

Bei zusammengesetzten Verben ("Verb-Partikel-Verbindungen", "Phrasal Verbs") wie *tow away* kann das Objekt (oben jeweils in Fettdruck) grundsätzlich sowohl zwischen Verb (*tow*) und Partikel (*away*) als auch hinter der Partikel stehen.
Faustregel: Ein langes und/oder betontes Objekt steht hinter dem zusammengesetzten Verb (1+2); ein kurzes und/oder unbetontes Objekt steht zwischen Verb und Partikel (3+4). Ist das Objekt ein Pronomen, so muß es zwischen Verb und Partikel stehen (4).

Change the following sentences as in the examples.

Have they sent out *cards or something*? (them) Have they sent *them* out?
Don't forget to bring *it* along. (the paper I gave you yesterday) Don't forget to bring along *the paper I gave you yesterday.*

a. My advice is: Give up *smoking and drinking*! (it)
b. Wherever did you pick *it* up? (that fascinating little book you sent us for Christmas)
c. Michael is taking out *the girl he gave evidence against in court last week.* (Susan)
d. Are you sure I have to fill in *all these idiotic forms*? (them all)
e. Why don't you read *it* out to us? (the letter Susan has written from Malta)
f. You'd better talk to the traffic warden before he writes out *a ticket.* (it)
g. How long does it take to get *it* back? (a car that has been towed away)
h. You can ring *her* up at this number. (the owner of the car)
i. We can't say anything before we've tried *it* out. (the new method suggested by them)

10M **Passiv. – Please translate.**

a. Was ist mit "gutter language" gemeint? b. Von wem werden diese Halstücher hergestellt? c. Jugendlichen unter achtzehn ist es nicht gestattet, ein Auto zu fahren. d. Mein Auto wurde abgeschleppt. e. Dieses Buch ist von den Kritikern gelobt worden. f. Diese Art von Buch könnte als für Jugendliche völlig ungeeignet angesehen werden.

10N **Saying the same thing differently**

Ersetzen Sie die schräggedruckten Satzteile durch Formulierungen, die etwa dasselbe bedeuten.

a. I *picked up* a parking ticket when I was in town this morning. b. How much *have you got* to pay? c. The police said my car was *causing an obstruction.* d. I only had a *bit of* shopping to do. e. When I *got back,* the car had *gone.* f. I *phoned* the police to find out where they'd taken my car. g. A traffic warden *issues* dozens of parking tickets every day. h. *Hold the line,* please. i. *As* the driver could not be found, the car was towed away. j. I only *parked* it there for a few minutes. k. *Maybe* it was a *bit* longer than I thought. l. You can collect your car from there *on production of* your driving licence and certificate of insurance.

10O **Ausdrücke mit Präpositionen**

about I'm ringing **about** my car *ich rufe wegen meines Wagens an* complain **about** something *sich über etwas beschweren*	**of** what do you think **of** it? *was hältst du davon?*
beside park **beside** a meter *neben einer Parkuhr parken*	**on** I didn't have any coins **on** me *ich hatte keine Münzen bei mir* **on** production of your driving licence *unter Vorlage Ihres Führerscheins*
near **near** a corner *in der Nähe einer Ecke*	**to** what's happened **to** my car? *was ist mit meinem Wagen geschehen?*

10P Dictation exercise

Hören Sie das Diktat vom Tonband und schreiben Sie dabei diejenigen Wörter nieder, die im folgenden Diktattext fehlen.

I .... I .... be long. After all, I .... wanted to .... a .... present for my wife – a scarf or something – at Selfridges in Oxford Street.
As .... all the parking meters .... taken, but .... was an .... space on the corner of Duke Street and Wigmore Street. That's .... I parked my car. It .... very much in the way ...., and I .... I would be back .... a .... minutes, so it .... matter.
As it happened, a traffic warden .... me parking my car, made a .... of the time, and later .... it to the police as ".......... an obstruction".
The police .... very quick – much quicker .... I was .... a scarf for my wife – and when I .... came back to .... I had parked the car, it was .... At first I .... it had been ...., but .... someone told me he .... it .... towed away. So I .... the police and was told my car had been .... to the car pound in Park Lane and I could .... it .... "on production of my driving .... and certificate of ....".
When I .... the scarf to my wife on her ...., I .... tell her how much it had .... me. I .... said: "This is not an .... scarf. .... it .... as .... as you .... think."

Grammatikübersicht IV

Substantiv

Genitiv

1 **Bildung und Aussprache**

Singular (-'s)		**Plural (-s')**	
Mr **Walker's** house	*Herrn Walkers Haus*	the **Walkers'** house	*das Haus der Walkers*
the **taxpayer's** money	*das Geld des Steuerzahlers*	the **taxpayers'** money	*das Geld der Steuerzahler*
the **boss's** behaviour	*das Verhalten des Chefs*	the **bosses'** behaviour	*das Verhalten der Chefs*

Unregelmäßige Plurale

a **children's** playground *ein Kinderspielplatz* **women's** occupations *Frauenberufe*

Eigennamen auf -s

Name	Häufigere geschriebene Form	Häufigere gesprochene Form
Briggs	Mike **Briggs'** garden	Mike **Briggs's** ['brigziz] garden
Williams	Susan **Williams'** wedding	Susan **Williams's** ['wiljəmziz] wedding

2 **Besonderheiten des Gebrauchs**

I bought it **at Foyle's / Macy's**. *ich habe es bei Foyle('s) / Macy('s) gekauft*
He's **at the travel agent's / at the butcher's**. *er ist im Reisebüro / beim Metzger*
She's **at the doctor's**. *sie ist beim Arzt*

He's **a friend of Jim's**. *er ist ein Freund von Jim* (*vgl.* he's a friend of **his** *er ist ein Freund von ihm*)

The casino is about **ten minutes' walk** away. *das Kasino ist etwa zehn Minuten Fußweg entfernt*

They hope they'll be able to buy a house **in a few years' time**. *in ein paar Jahren*

Artikel

3 **Wendungen mit the**

He visited us **the other day**. *er besuchte uns neulich*
We're having a little party **the weekend after next**. *übernächstes Wochenende*
He died **the next day**. *er starb am nächsten Tag*

a shop **in the High Street** (*aber* **in Oxford Street**, **in Old Street**, **in Piccadilly Circus** *etc.*)

entertainment **in the form of** party games *Unterhaltung in Form von Gesellschaftsspielen*

4 Englisch: ohne the – Deutsch: mit Artikel

Life is hard. *das Leben ist schwer*
What do **people** say? *was sagen die Leute?*
Things can only get better.
die Dinge können nur besser werden

He **lost touch** with her. *verlor den Kontakt mit ihr*
love **at first sight** *Liebe auf den ersten Blick*
He's still **at work**. *ist immer noch bei der Arbeit*

They work **in agriculture**.
sie arbeiten in der Landwirtschaft
after lunch *nach dem Mittagessen*
I was **in town**. *ich war in der Stadt*
get **out of bed** *aus dem Bett aufstehen*

in Switzerland / Turkey *in der Schweiz / Türkei*
on Christmas Day *am ersten Weihnachtsfeiertag*

5 Stellung von the bei all, half, twice, double

All the parking meters were taken. *alle Parkuhren waren besetzt*
He was talking **all the** time. *er redete die ganze Zeit*
He sold it at **half / twice / double the** price. *zum halben / "zweifachen" / doppelten Preis*

6 Wendungen mit a(n)

It's **a pity**. *es ist schade*
They got **a divorce**. *sie ließen sich scheiden*
take **an interest** in something
sich für etwas interessieren

He works 40 hours **a week**.
er arbeitet 40 Stunden in der Woche
It's **(a) quarter** to / past eight.
es ist Viertel vor / nach acht

He's caught **(a) cold**. *er hat sich erkältet*
I've got **a headache**. *ich habe Kopfschmerzen*
I've got **a pain** in my back.
ich habe Schmerzen im Rücken
He's got **a temperature**.
er hat Temperatur / Fieber

My father was **an architect**. *war Architekt*
I'm **a German citizen**. *bin deutscher Staatsbürger*

7 Stellung von a(n) bei half, quite, such, what

It took us **half an** hour. *wir brauchten eine halbe Stunde*
That's **quite a** difference. *das ist ein ziemlicher Unterschied*
He's **such an** unhappy man. *er ist so ein unglücklicher Mann*
What a surprise! *was für eine Überraschung!*

Adverb

8 Gebrauch des Adverbs

a1. What he saw made him [suspicious]. (suspicious = Adjektiv)

a2. She looked at him [suspiciously]. (suspiciously = Adverb)

b1. It's a [terrible] disease. (terrible = Adjektiv)

b2. He was [terribly] sick. (terribly = Adverb)

c. Ireland is [relatively] thinly populated. (relatively = Adverb)

d1. It is [unfortunate] that you will be away on that date. (unfortunate = Adjektiv)

d2. [Unfortunately,] it so happens that we'll be away on that date. (unfortunately = Adverb)

Während sich *Adjektive* auf Substantive (b1) bzw. Pronomen (a1, d1) beziehen, dienen *Adverbien* vor allem zur näheren Bestimmung von Verben (a2), Adjektiven (b2), Adverbien (c) und Sätzen (d2).
Die meisten englischen Adverbien werden durch Ableitung von Adjektiven gebildet:
Adjektiv: expensive (The flat is *expensive.*)
Adverb: expensively (The flat is *expensively* furnished.)

9 Bildung der -ly-Adverbien

Normalfall: Adjektiv + -ly = Adverb real – **really** pleasant – **pleasantly** cruel – **cruelly**	**-y wird meist zu -i-** easy – **easily** happy – **happily** lazy – **lazily**
Auf Mitlaut folgendes -le wird -ly possible – **possibly** terrible – **terribly** probable – **probably**	**-ic hängt -ally an** automatic – **automatically** basic – **basically** domestic – **domestically** *Ausnahme:* public – **publicly**

10 Ausnahme bei der Adverbbildung:

Adjektiv: good (His English is *good.*) → Adverb: well (He speaks English *well.*)

11 "Ursprüngliche" Adverbien

Außer den durch Anhängen von *-ly* aus Adjektiven gebildeten "abgeleiteten" Adverbien gibt es eine relativ kleine Gruppe von "ursprünglichen" Adverbien, die von der Form her keine Schwierigkeiten bieten, wohl aber hinsichtlich der bei ihnen gegebenen Stellungsmöglichkeiten (→ 12) Beachtung verdienen.
Zu den "ursprünglichen" Adverbien gehören: *again, already, also, always, even, ever, just, never, now, often, only, quite, rather, somehow, sometimes, soon, still, then, too, yet.*

12 Stellung des Adverbs

a. Im Englischen tritt das Adverb – anders als im Deutschen – in der Regel nicht zwischen Verb und Objekt. Es steht statt dessen häufig vor dem Verb:

	Adverb	Verb	Objekt
He	**also**	collected	American folk songs.
We	**always**	have	a spare bed for you.
His old friends	**hardly ever**	visit	him.
He	**certainly**	didn't show	it.
She	**probably**	picked up	some infection.

Vgl. dagegen im Deutschen:
Er sammelte *auch* / *Auch* sammelte er amerikanische Volkslieder.
Wir haben *immer* ein Bett für dich frei.
Seine alten Freunde besuchen ihn *fast nie.*

b. Ebenfalls typisch ist die Stellung des Adverbs zwischen modalem Hilfsverb (+ *n't* / *not*) und Hauptverb:

	Modales Hilfsverb	**Adverb**	Verb	
That	could	**only**	happen	in America.
He	couldn't	**possibly**	get	to the airport in time.
He	can't	**even**	count.	
Schools	must	**obviously**	take	most of the blame.

c. "Wie"-Adverbien ("Adverbien der Art und Weise") werden meist nachgestellt:

He invested his winnings	**wisely**.
I think you didn't understand him	**correctly**.
Please get me a doctor	**quickly**.
She knows the bride and her family quite	**well**.

Pronomen

13 **Gebrauch der adjektivischen (= vor einem Substantiv stehenden) Possessivpronomen**

I have a little mole on **my** left shoulder and a small scar on **my** right knee.
auf der linken Schulter . . . auf dem rechten Knie
I helped her to **her** feet. *auf die Füße*
I've got a pain in **my** back. *im Rücken*
He had **his** hands in **his** pockets. *die Hände in den Taschen*

Das Possessivpronomen steht abweichend vom Deutschen bei Dingen, die eng zu einer Person gehören, also Körperteilen, Kleidungsstücken usw.
Ausnahmen:
The dog bit her in *the* arm. (Subjekt des Satzes und "Besitzer" des Armes sind nicht dieselbe Person!)
Judy has been giving him *the* cold shoulder recently.
You must keep *an* eye on her.

14 **Die substantivischen (= alleinstehenden) Possessivpronomen**

he's a friend	of	**mine**	*von mir*
		yours	*von dir / Ihnen / euch*
		his	*von ihm*
		hers	*von ihr*
		ours	*von uns*
		theirs	*von ihnen*

Weitere Beispiele:
We heard a loud noise in the room next to **ours**.
Australians are beginning to accept people like us who have a background different from **theirs**.
die einen Werdegang haben, der anders ist als ihrer
Some customer of **ours** is complaining about our product. *irgendein Kunde von uns*

15 **-self-Pronomen: verstärkend gebraucht ("selbst")**

I	**myself**	didn't see it	*ich selbst*
you	**yourself**	didn't see it	*du / Sie selbst*
he	**himself**	didn't see it	*er selbst*
she	**herself**	didn't see it	*sie selbst*
the house	**itself**	is very pleasant	*das Haus selbst*
we	**ourselves**	didn't see it	*wir selbst*
you	**yourselves**	didn't see it	*ihr / Sie selbst*
they	**themselves**	didn't see it	*sie selbst*

Weitere Beispiele:
I'm a mother of four **myself**.
ich bin selber Mutter von vier Kindern
There are prizes for **yourself** and for your boss. *für Sie selbst und Ihren Chef*
Dennis **himself** doesn't remember much about that night at the Green Banana.
They tried it out **themselves**.
sie probierten es selber aus

16 Relativpronomen

Relativsätze (= Beifügungssätze) können durch folgende Relativpronomen eingeleitet werden:

Who	A person **who commits a traffic offence** usually has to pay a fine. *der ein Verkehrsdelikt / einen Verkehrsverstoß begeht*
Whose	A person **whose job it is to check cars parked at parking meters** is called a traffic warden. *dessen Aufgabe es ist, an Parkuhren geparkte Autos zu kontrollieren*
Which	Can you suggest ways **in which this problem might be overcome**? *auf welche dieses Problem überwunden werden könnte*
That	Money is the only thing **that really counts.** *das einzige, was wirklich zählt*

Notwendige (→ GIII10) Relativsätze haben oft kein Relativpronomen, wenn dieses Relativpronomen Objekt – nicht Subjekt – wäre:

There is the man **(who) I saw**. (*Who* = Objekt. "Wen habe ich gesehen?")

There is the man **who saw me**. (*Who* = Subjekt. "Wer hat mich gesehen?")

Weitere Beispiele:

Thanks a lot for the fascinating little book **(that / which) you sent us for Christmas.**
das du mir zu Weihnachten geschickt hast

Let me quote something **(that / which) Mark Twain wrote**. *was Mark Twain geschrieben hat*

They could not find the kind of work **(that) they had been trained for** / the kind of work **for which they had been trained**[1]. *für die sie ausgebildet worden waren*

The future is something **(that) Dennis refuses to think about / about which Dennis refuses to think**[1].
an das / woran zu denken Dennis sich weigert

[1] Nach Präpositionen (hier *for* und *about*) kann nur *which* – nicht *that* – stehen.

Verb

17 Gebrauch der Zeiten für Gegenwart und Vergangenheit (Übersicht)

Präsens einfach **Präsens Verlaufsform** ("gerade", "jetzt", "vorübergehend")	They **live** in Leeds. They **are living** in Leeds.	*sie wohnen in Leeds* *sie wohnen (z. Zt.) in L.*
Vergangenheit einfach **Vergangenheit Verlaufsform** ("damals gerade / vorübergehend")	They **lived** in Leeds. They **were living** in Leeds.	*sie wohnten in Leeds* *sie wohnten (damals gerade / noch) in Leeds*
Perfekt (Handl. abgeschlossen) **Perfekt** (Handlung begann in der Vergangenheit und dauert noch an)	They **have moved** to Leeds. They **have been living** in Leeds for five years / since 1974.	*sie sind nach L. gezogen* *sie wohnen seit fünf Jahren / seit 1974 in Leeds*

Plusquamperfekt (Handlung vor best. Zeitpunkt i. d. Vergangenheit bereits abgeschlossen)	When I first met them, they **had just moved** to Leeds.	*waren sie gerade nach Leeds gezogen*
Plusquamperfekt (Handlung dauert zu best. Zeitpkt. in der Vergangenheit noch an)	When I first met them, they **had been living** in L. for six months.	*wohnten sie seit einem halben Jahr in Leeds*

18 **Futur** (→ 1M)

Es gibt im wesentlichen fünf Möglichkeiten, zukünftige Handlungen auszudrücken:

a. Will + Infinitiv ("neutrale Zukunft")

She **will** / She'**ll see** him tomorrow. *sie wird ihn morgen besuchen*

b. Be going to + Infinitiv (Betonung von Absicht oder Gewißheit)

She's **going to see** him tomorrow. *(Absicht:) sie wird ihn morgen besuchen*
Prices **are going to rise**. *(Gewißheit:) die Preise werden steigen*

c. Be + -ing-Form (Handlung vorgesehen, geplant)

She's **seeing** him tomorrow. *(etwas "direkter, salopper" als d:) sie besucht ihn morgen*

d. Will be + -ing-Form (Handlung vorgesehen, geplant, "normaler Lauf der Ereignisse")

She **will** / She'**ll be seeing** him tomorrow. *sie wird ihn morgen besuchen*

e. Einfache Form des Präsens ("Fahrplanzukunft")

She / Her train **leaves** at ten fifteen. *sie / ihr Zug fährt um zehn Uhr fünfzehn ab*

19 **Bedingungssätze: Die drei Grundtypen** (→ 13H)

Typ 1

If-Satz: Präsens	**Hauptsatz: will + Infinitiv**
If we **leave** at two, *wenn wir um zwei abfahren,*	we **will** / we'**ll get** there at five. *werden wir um fünf dort ankommen*

Typ 2

If-Satz: Vergangenheitsform	**Hauptsatz: would + Infinitiv**
If we **left** at two, *wenn wir um zwei abführen,*	we **would** / we'**d get** there at five. *würden wir um fünf dort ankommen*

Typ 3

If-Satz: had + Partizip Perfekt	Hauptsatz: would have + Partizip Perfekt
If we **had left** at two, *wenn wir um zwei abgefahren wären,*	we **would have got** there at five. *wären wir um fünf dort angekommen*

20 Indirekte Rede (→ GIII18, 5H)

Direkte Rede		The play	**is**	no good.	*das Stück taugt nichts*
Indirekte Rede	He **said**	the play	**was**	no good.	*er sagte, das Stück tauge nichts*

Steht das die indirekte Rede einleitende Berichtsverb in der Vergangenheitsform (hier: *said*), so wird das Verb des abhängigen, berichteten Satzes in der Regel um eine Zeitstufe in die Vergangenheit "gerückt" (hier: *is* → *was*). Die folgenden Beispiele liefern dafür weitere typische Belege:

a. "The room booked by you **has** been given to someone else."
They were told that the room booked by them **had** been given to someone else.

b. "He **died** about a week later."
I was told that he **(had) died** about a week later.

c. "Mr Cole **was** very independent."
Neighbours said that Mr Cole **had been** very independent.

d. "Construction **will** take five years."
It was estimated that construction **would** take five years.

e. "**Can** I take you out?"
He asked her if he **could** take her out.

Zu b und c: Da das Plusquamperfekt (*had died, had been*) als "umständlich" empfunden wird, behält man an seiner Stelle häufig die Vergangenheitsform bei, wenn die zeitlichen Bezüge auch so unmißverständlich sind. In c wäre die Vergangenheitsform allerdings mißverständlich: *Neighbours said that Mr Cole was very independent* würde aussagen, daß Mr Cole noch lebt: "Die Nachbarn sagten, daß Herr Cole sehr unabhängig / selbständig sei."

21 Passiv

Übersicht: Typische Passivkonstruktionen

Präsens einfach **Präsens Verlaufsform**	The plans **are** often **changed**. The plans **are being changed**.	*werden oft geändert* *werden (gerade) geändert*
Vergangenheit einfach **Vergangenheit Verlaufsform**	The plans **were changed**. The plans **were being changed**.	*wurden geändert* *wurden (gerade) geändert*

Perfekt	The plans **have been changed**.	*sind geändert worden.*
Plusquamperfekt	The plans **had been changed**.	*waren geändert worden*
Will-Futur	The plans **will be changed**.	*werden geändert werden*
Nach modalen Hilfsverben	The plans **can** / **must** / **should be changed**.	*können / müssen / sollten geändert werden*
Nach have to	The plans **had to be changed**.	*mußten geändert werden*
To-Infinitiv	It's time for the plans **to be changed**.	*daß die Pläne geändert werden*
-ing-Form	Is there any possibility of the plans **being changed**?	*(irgend)eine Möglichkeit, daß die Pläne geändert werden*

Frage nach dem Urheber

Who were the plans changed **by**? *von wem wurden die Pläne geändert?*

Persönliches Passiv (direktes Objekt als Subjekt der Passivkonstruktion)

They **told** me that he had died about a week later.
I **was told** that he had died about a week later. *man sagte mir*

To-Infinitiv

22 **To-Infinitiv nach bestimmten Verben** (→ GIII25)

They decided / intended / liked / offered / planned / preferred / tried / used / wanted **to do** it alone.
She arranged / expected / hoped / promised **to meet** him in London.
She forgot / refused **to pay** the bill.
The unemployment rate began / continued / started **to drop**.
He came / managed **to understand** everything.
The plans proved / seemed **to be** very difficult.
Do you happen **to know** how much it costs?

Weitere Verben, die häufig mit nachfolgendem *to*-Infinitiv gebraucht werden: *agree, ask, expect, need, wish.*

Anmerkung: *begin, continue, like, prefer, start* können auch mit nachfolgender *-ing*-Form gebraucht werden (→ GIV26).

23 To-Infinitiv nach bestimmten Substantiven (→ GIII23)

It's a crime / pleasure / sin **to do** that.
Would you have the courage **to do** it?
We won't have enough time **to do** it.
Then it was my turn **to buy** drinks.

Weitere Substantive, die häufig mit nachfolgendem *to*-Infinitiv gebraucht werden: *chance, freedom, habit, means, occasion, plan, reason, right, way.*

24 To-Infinitiv nach bestimmten Adjektiven

It was dangerous / difficult / easy / good / hard / important / impossible / right / stupid / unfair **to change** that.
We were delighted / disturbed / glad / happy / interested / sorry **to hear** that.
She was (un)able **to lift** him up.
I would be interested **to know** what you think.
It wouldn't be prepared / ready **to pay** more.
The Olympic Games are due **to open** on 19 July.
They are (un)likely / sure **to ask** that sort of question.

25 To-Infinitiv nach Verb + Objekt

We allowed / asked / encouraged / expected / invited / wanted **her to enter** the competition.
She got / helped / told **him to fill in** the necessary forms.
If you apply for a loan, the bank requires **you to fill in** a detailed questionnaire.
She employs **another woman to do** the housework for her.
Would you like / prefer **us to arrange** accommodation?
What led **the police to believe** that Mr Cole had been dead for five months?

Bei bestimmten Verben kommt das Passiv der Verb-Objekt-Infinitiv-Konstruktion häufig vor:

		Verb	Objekt	Infinitiv	
Aktiv	The bank	**requires**	**you**	**to fill in**	a detailed questionnaire.
Passiv	**You**	**are required**		**to fill in**	a detailed questionnaire.
	Subjekt	Verb		Infinitiv	

Weitere Beispiele des Passivs der Verb-Objekt-Infinitiv-Konstruktion:
She was asked / encouraged / expected / invited **to enter** the competition.
He is allowed / permitted **to drive** a car.
The police were led **to believe** that he didn't die a natural death.
This is claimed **to be** the warmest and clearest water in the whole of the Mediterranean.

26 -ing-Form nach bestimmten Verben

When did he begin / continue / finish / give up / go on / start **studying**?
Do you enjoy / like / prefer **reading** poetry?
I don't mind / remember **telling** you how I did it.
Just fancy / imagine **meeting** your husband that way!
I can't help **wondering** how he spent his school years.

Anmerkung: *begin, continue, like, prefer, start* können auch mit nachfolgendem *to*-Infinitiv gebraucht werden (→ GIV22).

27 Verb + Präposition + -ing-Form

We're looking forward **to seeing** you on the 20th.
I'm thinking **of going** back to work at the factory.

28 Substantiv + Präposition + -ing-Form

Do you think there's any chance **of getting** a job?
Malta has the advantage **of being** an English-speaking country.
That's certainly one way **of solving** the problem.
After an hour **of pottering** about in the garden he had tea with his wife.
He didn't take time off for fear **of being** sacked.

29 Adjektiv + Präposition + -ing-Form

A textbook published in 1840 can't be suitable **for learning** English today.
I'm not fond **of spending** the day pottering about in the garden.

-ing-Konstruktion als adverbiale Bestimmung

30 -ing mit vorangehender Präposition oder Konjunktion

After eating a good meal, we went to the theatre. *nachdem wir gut gegessen hatten*
What did they do **after discovering the body**? *nachdem sie die Leiche entdeckt hatten*
He met his wife **while travelling in Italy**. *während er Italien bereiste / auf einer Italienreise*
You should know that **when travelling in Quebec**. *wenn Sie in Quebec reisen*
He parked his car beside a meter **without putting a coin in**. *ohne eine Münze einzustecken*
Instead of phoning the emergency service, she went and fetched the man's wife.
anstatt den Notdienst anzurufen
On wanting to leave the bathroom, he found that he could not open the door.
als er das Badezimmer verlassen wollte
In defending the use of such books, teachers point out that they have been praised by critics.
wenn / indem sie den Gebrauch dieser Bücher verteidigen

31 -ing ohne vorangehende Präposition oder Konjunktion

I staggered around **holding my foot**. *und hielt mir den Fuß*
He's still at school, **working for his exams just now**. *und arbeitet gerade für sein Examen*

I am writing this **sitting by the side of the swimming pool**. *während ich am Rand des . . . sitze*

Knowing what a success your marriage has been so far, we can only wish you MANY HAPPY RETURNS. *da wir wissen, was für ein Erfolg eure Ehe bis jetzt gewesen ist*
I'd have guessed where your car was anyway, **knowing what traffic wardens are like nowadays**. *da ich weiß, wie die Parkuhrkontrolleure heutzutage sind*
Being migrants with a poor knowledge of English, they could not find the kind of work they had been trained for. *da sie Einwanderer mit schlechten Englischkenntnissen waren*

Judging from the letter, their holiday has been very pleasant so far. *dem Brief nach zu urteilen*

Modale Hilfsverben und Spezialverben

Modale Hilfsverben: Ersatzformen für Vergangenheit und Zukunft

32 Can – be able to

Gegenwart	I **can't** join them.	*kann nicht*
Vergangenheit	I **wasn't able / was unable to** join them.	*konnte nicht*
Zukunft	I **won't be able / I'll be unable to** join them.	*werde nicht können*

33 Must – have to

Gegenwart	We **must** change our plans.	*müssen unsere Pläne ändern*
Vergangenheit	We **had to** change our plans.	*mußten unsere Pläne ändern*
Zukunft	We'll **have to** change our plans.	*werden unsere Pläne ändern müssen*

34 Modales Hilfsverb + Infinitiv des Perfekts

He **can't have done** it. *er kann es nicht getan haben*
That **could not have happened** here. *das hätte hier nicht passieren können*
He **may have died** five months ago. *er kann (schon) vor fünf Monaten gestorben sein / es kann sein, daß er (schon) vor fünf Monaten gestorben ist*
They **must have seen** the old man. *sie müssen den alten Mann gesehen haben*
She **should have phoned** the emergency service. *sie hätte den Notdienst anrufen sollen*

35 Frageanhängsel (→ 10J)

Bejahte Aussage – verneintes Frageanhängsel:

You live here, **don't you**? *Sie wohnen hier, nicht wahr?*

Verneinte Aussage – bejahtes Frageanhängsel:

You don't live here, **do you**? *Sie wohnen nicht hier, oder doch?*

Verkürzte Anschlußfrage (→ AB1 26K):

I like him, **don't you**? *ich mag ihn, Sie nicht? / mir gefällt er, Ihnen nicht?*

11K **Have + Objekt + Partizip Perfekt** (→ GIII38)

They	**had**	**parking meters**	**installed.**	*sie ließen Parkuhren installieren*
He	**had**	**the text**	**translated.**	*er ließ den Text übersetzen*
Can I	**have**	**the window**	**opened?**	*kann ich das Fenster geöffnet bekommen?*

Make sentences as in the examples above.

He I want to I'll The boss The police They Why do you want to	had have	all the plans an information sheet everything the book the door the leather these shirts your dog	(arrange). (change). (destroy). (draw up). (iron). (make into gloves). (open). (send under separate cover).

"I wonder . . . could we have a window opened?"

11L **Have + Objekt + Partizip Perfekt**

Please translate.

a. Sie ließen den Toaster reparieren.
b. Er ließ einen Platz in der Morgenmaschine buchen.
c. Die Polizei ließ den Wagen abschleppen.
d. Er ließ Abschriften an alle Mitglieder des Ausschusses schicken.
e. Ich werde die Rechnung stornieren lassen.
f. Wir müssen einige Aufnahmen / Fotos machen lassen.
g. Ich werde den Brief übersetzen lassen müssen.

11 M **Relativsätze** (→ GIV16)

> I have a friend .who. drives a Mini.
> This is the gentleman whose car has been stolen.
> The methods by which our children are taught are very progressive.
> Here are a few things .that. may be useful.
> I liked the book . – . . you sent me for Christmas.

Complete the following sentences, leaving the relative pronoun out where possible.

a. Is that the tea set . . . . . you bought in London? b. Is that the customer . . . . . bought the tea set? c. Are those the plates . . . . . are cracked? d. Do you think there really are people . . . . . can predict the future? e. The old man was seen by dozens of people, both pedestrians and motorists . . . . . stopped at a nearby shop . . . . . was still open. f. Malta is an English-speaking country . . . . . institutions and everyday life resemble England's in many ways. g. In 1965 the state government . . . . . started the project lost the election. h. I'm afraid there's nothing . . . . . I can do, sir. i. The *C* stands for *Chaud,* . . . . . is French for "hot". j. The car was parked there for over 35 minutes according to the traffic warden . . . . . reported it. k. A large downtown department store hired an "anti-meter maid", ... job it was to make the same rounds as the meter maid and put coins in all the meters . . . . . were about to expire. l. The plans . . . . . had been made by the architect proved to be very difficult and had to be changed again and again. m. Fun is the only thing . . . . . money can't buy. n. What do you think of the way . . . . . they have solved the parking problem? o. There's a wonderful prize for the lucky girl . . . . . wins the title. p. New Zealand is a combination of Norway and Switzerland, both of . . . . . I like very much. q. You can't have a secretary . . . . . is untidy.

11 N **Saying the same thing differently**

Ersetzen Sie die schräggedruckten Satzteile durch Formulierungen, die etwa dasselbe bedeuten.

a. They decided to have parking meters installed in the *downtown area.* b. We usually do our shopping at the *downtown stores.* c. The new parking meters *turned out* to be anything but profitable. d. He *made a discovery.* e. Wait a *minute.* f. You *should* know that when *travelling* in Quebec. g. *He had no difficulty in explaining* it. h. She *is very efficient.*

11O To-Infinitiv, -ing-Form oder Präposition + -ing-Form? (→ 11J)

Put in the correct form of the verb in brackets (to infinitive, -ing form or preposition + -ing form).

a. He refuses (think) about the future. b. I remember (see) him at the club the day before it happened. c. What reasons do the separatists have (want) to leave the union? d. I'm thinking (go) back to work at the canteen. e. An "anti-meter maid" was hired to put coins in all the meters that were about (expire). f. A book of English dialogues published in 1840 can't be suitable (learn) English today. g. Fancy (marry) the policeman who booked you for (cause) an accident. h. I cannot help (wonder) how these illiterate youngsters spent their school years. i. Are you permitted (drive) a car here? j. This questionnaire contains the questions most likely (be) asked.

11P Translate as in the examples.

The costs **rose and rose**. *die Kosten stiegen und stiegen / stiegen immer weiter*
Parking became **more and more difficult**. *das Parken wurde immer schwieriger*
The traffic wardens are getting **worse and worse**. *werden immer schlimmer*

a. Die Fernsehprogramme werden immer schlechter.
b. (Die) Taschenrechner werden immer billiger.
c. Der Film wurde immer interessanter.
d. Immer mehr alte Leute müssen in Altenheimen leben.
e. Immer mehr Leute ziehen in die Vororte.
f. Er arbeitet immer mehr und verdient immer weniger.

11Q Dictation exercise

Hören Sie das Diktat vom Tonband und schreiben Sie dabei diejenigen Wörter nieder, die im folgenden Diktattext fehlen.

When the town fathers of Whitehorse, Canada, had parking meters .... in the downtown ...., these .... simply .... by motorists. The town fathers had no .... but to .... an energetic meter maid, who had to .... the streets checking the meters and .... tickets to parking ....

The meter maid was so .... that more and more customers .... away from the downtown stores and did .... shopping at a shopping .... outside the town.
To .... their customers from doing .... shopping ...., a large downtown department store .... an "anti-meter maid", ... job it was to make the .... round as the meter maid and put .... in all the meters that .... about to ....

11 R **Ausdrücke mit Präpositionen**

about
think **about** a problem
über ein Problem nachdenken

as
they regard English **as** their language
sie betrachten Engl. als ihre Sprache
A is **as** large **as** B
A ist so groß wie B

at
at the same time
zu gleicher Zeit / gleichzeitig
scream **at** somebody *jem. anschreien*

from
stay away **from** a place
einem Ort fernbleiben
prevent somebody **from** doing something
jem. daran hindern, etwas zu tun
A is different **from** B
A ist anders als B

in
he had no difficulty **in** explaining it
er hatte keine Schwierigkeiten, es zu erklären

of
ways **of** solving a problem
Möglichkeiten, ein Problem zu lösen
in the Canadian town **of** Whitehorse
in der kanadischen Stadt Whitehorse
think **of** something *an etwas denken*

to
complain **to** somebody
sich bei jemandem beschweren
issue tickets **to** parking offenders
Parksündern Strafzettel ausstellen
a welcome addition **to** the town's funds
eine willkommene Bereicherung der städtischen Geldmittel

with
be pleased **with** something
über etwas erfreut sein

12E Give answers as in the examples.

Our local supermarket is quite cheap, isn't it? (most of the shops in town) Yes, it's cheaper than most of the shops in town.
Superwash is rather expensive, isn't it? (the other washing powders) Yes, it's more expensive than the other washing powders.

a. She's quite happy now, isn't she? (she's ever been before)
b. The jumbo size is quite practical, isn't it? (the smaller size)
c. The Sydney Opera House is quite beautiful, isn't it? (any other arts centre I know)
d. Her working day is rather long, isn't it? (her husband's)
e. Parking is rather difficult here, isn't it? (where you live)
f. What she did was quite sensible, wasn't it? (what her husband did)
g. It's quite a good job, isn't it? (my previous job)
h. Meat is rather dear at Harper's, isn't it? (any of the other shops)
i. The situation is rather alarming, isn't it? (most people think)
j. He drinks quite a lot, doesn't he? (anyone else in the family)
k. You're feeling rather bad, aren't you? (when I came an hour ago)

12F Frageanhängsel (→ 10J)

That's against the law, ... That's against the law, isn't it?

Add question tags to the following sentences. ꝏ

a. That was a few days ago, ... b. You paid 20p, ... c. That's a large loaf, ... d. Supermarkets buy things in large quantities, ... e. They can sell them cheaper than large stores, ... f. Your husband didn't know you had it on your shopping list, ... g. Shopping around takes time, ... h. You aren't in a hurry, ... i. You're a pensioner, ... j. Pensioners have all the time in the world, ... k. It's not difficult to compare prices, ... l. You can't carry all that information around in your head, ... m. The packets are not the same size, ... n. You haven't got a pocket calculator on you, ... o. So there wasn't any saving at all on the jumbo, ...

12G **Some – any** (→ GIII11)

a. I had **some** coins on me.

b. Have you got **any** coins on you?

c. I haven't got **any** coins on me.
They did it without **any** difficulty.
We have hardly **any** money.

"We have hardly any money left."

Grundregel:
Some steht in bejahten Aussagesätzen (a).
Any steht in Fragesätzen (b) und verneinten (bzw. durch Wörter wie *without* oder *hardly* "quasi verneinten") Aussagesätzen (c).
Besonderheiten:

Why don't you get yourself **something** to drink?
Can I have **some** sort of air conditioning in the room?

Some steht auch in Fragesätzen oder verneinten Sätzen, wenn diese einen bejahenden Sinn haben (Einladung, Aufforderung, Erwartung einer bejahenden Antwort usw.)

Put in some or any.

a. The pianist at the pub sang . . . . . nice old songs for us. b. We must do . . . . .-thing to get the costs under control. c. Do you feel . . . . . pain? d. Did . . . . .one see it being towed away? e. We've never had . . . . . complaints. f. I don't know . . . . .body who is bilingual. g. You know me well enough to say "no" without . . . . . fuss. h. Hardly . . . . .body knows that. i. Why don't you eat . . . . . cherries. They're nice and sweet. j. Can I have . . . . .thing to drink, please? k. Why don't you ask . . . . .one at the Patent Office? l. Is there . . . . . saving on the jumbo size? m. I don't want to have . . . . .thing to do with it. n. I ate very little, but I lost hardly . . . . . weight. o. Didn't she marry . . . . .body we know? p. I had no idea she was getting married. Did they send out cards or . . . . .thing? q. Can you get us . . . . . theatre tickets, please? r. We can't do . . . . .thing to help them, I'm afraid. s. Why doesn't the Government do . . . . . thing about it? t. Is . . . . .-thing wrong? You don't look very well.

12H "Man"

"Man" wird im Englischen häufig durch *you* oder *one* ausgedrückt:

You have to have a brain like a computer to be able to work that out.
man muß ein Gehirn wie ein Computer haben

We've included everything **one** can possibly want in an up-to-the-minute hotel.
alles, was man sich nur wünschen kann

Oft entspricht dem deutschen "man" im Englischen auch eine Passivkonstruktion:

I was told that he died about a week later. *man sagte mir*
This problem **can't be solved**. *dies Problem kann man nicht lösen*

"Isn't it terrible when you've nothing to do?"

Please translate.

a. Was macht man, wenn man in Eile ist?
b. Es ist schrecklich, wenn man nichts zu tun hat.
c. Wenn man seinen Wagen in der Mitte der Straße parkt, wird er abgeschleppt.
d. Was tut man, wenn man nicht imstande ist, seinen Haushalt selbst zu führen ("seinen eigenen Haushalt zu führen")?
e. Ein Führerschein ist ein Dokument, das besagt, daß man ein Auto fahren darf.
f. Der Lärm bringt einen um den Verstand.
g. Wie kann man solche Tragödien verhindern?
h. Man fand bis zu fünf Monate alte Briefe und Zeitungen hinter der Haustür.
i. In welches Krankenhaus hat man ihn gebracht?

12I Hochleistungswort of (→ GII3, AB1 25M)

the quality **of** this washing powder the price **of** this article	*die Qualität dieses Waschpulvers* *der Preis dieses Artikels*
the republic **of** Malta in the Canadian town **of** Whitehorse	*die Republik Malta* *in der kanadischen Stadt Whitehorse*
a tin **of** salmon a loaf **of** bread	*eine Büchse Lachs* *ein Laib Brot*

Please translate, using phrases with of.

a. Ich verließ die Grundschule im Alter von zehn (Jahren). b. Sie verbrachten den Rest ihres Lebens in einem Bungalow an der See. c. Er war der Held der Nation. d. Können Sie mir die Nummer des Queen's Hotel geben? e. Ich habe gute Französischkenntnisse. f. Quebec City ist die Hauptstadt der Provinz Quebec. g. Malta ist Mitglied des Europarats. h. Die Insel Gozo ist ein Teil der Republik Malta. i. Sie kaufte zwei Pfund Äpfel und eine Flasche Tomaten-Ketchup.

12J Dictation exercise

.... made by the same .... is sold at different prices by different shops. A .... that sells at 20p at a small shop may cost as .... as 15p at a supermarket.

The supermarket is .... cheaper .... the corner shop because it .... things in large .... at great .... But it also happens that an .... costs less at a small shop .... it .... at a large store. So it .... to shop ...., but many .... are unable to do that because they are too ....

.... prices is .... as long as you have things that are .... identical. If, for .... , a .... brand of .... ketchup costs 34p per .... at shop A and $28\frac{1}{2}$p at shop B, then you .... that B is cheaper .... A. But what do you do when there are six different brands of washing powder on the .... at the supermarket and they are all different prices? To .... which washing powder is the best .... for money, you have to .... what .... in quality, if any, there are and .... the .... are all the same .... Even if you had that information, it .... still be .... to say .... which washing powder is the best ....

12K **Listening comprehension** ꝏ

Listen to the text on tape and decide whether the following statements are True (T) or Not True (NT).

(New words: traffic jam = Verkehrsstau; exhaust fumes = Abgase; unload = entladen; shake apart = durch Erschütterungen zerstören; on the contrary = im Gegenteil.)

a. The member of the Town Planning Committee starts by describing the time when Henley had no traffic problems.
b. Some of the streets in Henley are too narrow for two lorries side by side.
c. The first parking meters were installed two years ago.
d. Nobody knew anything about the council's plans until this meeting.
e. The parking facilities in Castle Street will be improved by making the car park there bigger.

f. The speaker from Hurley, a village outside Henley, has often got stuck in a traffic jam.
g. She thinks the air in Henley is very dirty.
h. She thinks stopping lorries using the town centre will solve the traffic problem.
i. She thinks it's too far from the High Street to the car park for people with heavy shopping bags.
j. She thinks the council's plan for a traffic-free precinct will mean there still aren't enough parking facilities.

k. Cyril Ford owns a big new shopping centre in Henley, next to a bank.
l. A lorry brings him a delivery at least once a day.
m. Delivery lorries can park right outside Cyril Ford's place in Castle Street.
n. Cyril Ford thinks through traffic should be allowed through Henley before 9 in the morning and after 5 in the afternoon.
o. Cyril Ford thinks he and the other shopkeepers will lose customers if the town centre is made into a traffic-free precinct.

p. Cyril Ford suggests that only part of the town centre should be made into a traffic-free precinct and that parking meters should be installed in the rest of the streets in the centre.
q. Cyril Ford thinks people who work in Henley can be encouraged to use the car park outside the town centre.
r. The last speaker says the foundations and other parts of the old buildings in Henley are being damaged by the traffic.
s. She thinks the scheme Mr Ford suggests will only partly improve the present situation.
t. She says Mr Ford will earn more money if everybody accepts the original plan.

13H **Bedingungssätze** (→ GIV19)

Typ 1
If the dog **dies**, she **will be** very sad.
wenn der Hund stirbt, wird sie sehr traurig sein / ist sie sehr traurig

Typ 2
If the dog **died**, she **would be** very sad.
wenn der Hund stürbe, würde sie sehr traurig sein / wäre sie sehr traurig

Typ 3
If the dog **had died**, she **would have been** very sad.
wenn der Hund gestorben wäre, wäre sie sehr traurig gewesen

Bei Typ 3 (→ 9F–9G) handelt es sich um eine besonders schwierige Art von Bedingungssatz. Beachten Sie die englischen Entsprechungen von "hätte" und "wäre" in den folgenden Bedingungssätzen vom Typ 3:

If I **had** found it, I **would have** given it to you.
wenn ich es gefunden hätte, hätte ich es dir gegeben

If they **had** gone on foot, they **would have** got there sooner.
wenn sie zu Fuß gegangen wären, wären sie eher angekommen

Im Satzteil mit *if*: *hätte / wäre = had.*
Im Satzteil ohne *if*: *hätte / wäre = would have.*

Please translate.

a. Was hätten wir gemacht, wenn der Schäferhund das Kind angegriffen hätte? b. Was hätten Sie getan, wenn Sie an Herrn Duffields Stelle gewesen wären? c. Er wäre sehr (*absolutely*) wütend gewesen, wenn das passiert wäre. d. Wenn der Hund nicht einen neuen Besitzer gefunden hätte, wäre er getötet worden. e. Wenn du ihm einen Drink spendiert (*buy*) hättest, wäre er nicht so aggressiv geworden. f. Wenn wir jünger gewesen wären, (dann) hätte das Geld unser Leben verändert. g. Wenn Dennis Bryan vernünftiger gewesen wäre, (dann) hätte er seine Frau nicht verlassen. h. Wenn Dennis nicht Judy kennengelernt hätte, hätte er sich nicht von seiner Frau scheiden lassen. i. Wenn er bei seiner Frau geblieben wäre, (dann) wäre er kein Alkoholiker geworden.

May zum Ausdruck der Möglichkeit / Wahrscheinlichkeit:
TV **may** be dangerous for young children.
es kann sein, daß . . . gefährlich ist / vielleicht ist . . . gefährlich
Even a very small dog **may** bark so loudly that all hell breaks loose.
kann so laut bellen / bellt vielleicht so laut / es kann sein, daß . . . so laut bellt

May zum Ausdruck der Erlaubnis:
You **may** park here. *Sie dürfen / können hier parken*
The children **may** use the swimming pool if they like. *dürfen / können das Schwimmbecken benutzen, wenn sie wollen*
May I ask you a personal question? *darf ich Ihnen eine persönliche Frage stellen?*

Change the following sentences, using may.

It's possible that people will invite you to spend the night.
Perhaps / Maybe people will invite you to spend the night.
People *may* invite you to spend the night.

Am I allowed / permitted to use your phone?
Have I got the right to use your phone?
May I use your phone?

a. It's possible that this is just the right thing for you. b. Am I allowed to visit him in hospital? c. You're permitted to park your car here for a limited time. d. Perhaps you will find the following words and expressions useful. e. It's possible that a new car of this type will cost you £3,000. f. Perhaps I can get back into my old job at Empire Machines. g. A court has the right to order the destruction of an animal if it would be cruel to keep it alive. h. People who are in despair always have the possibility of ringing The Samaritans. i. Is it possible for tickets to be booked in advance? j. A policeman has the right to cause an injured animal to be destroyed. k. Maybe he's still sleeping. l. Perhaps it has been towed away. m. Under the Protection of Animals Act of 1911 it is forbidden to keep an animal without food or water. (Passiv!)

13J **"Soll" – "sollte" (shall – be to – should / ought to)** (→ GV15)

Shall I look after the dog while you're away? *soll ich . . .?*
Shall I get you some when I go downtown? *soll ich . . .?*

The money **is to** be used for the dog. *soll für den Hund verwendet werden*
I **was to** spend the night at a hotel near the airport.
sollte . . . verbringen (das war so vorgesehen)

I think you **ought to / should** see a doctor. *du solltest einen Arzt aufsuchen*
We **ought to / should** have left earlier. *hätten eher abfahren sollen*

Beachten Sie folgenden Unterschied:
He *ought to / should* do it at once. (*sollte = es wäre richtig, wenn . . .*)
He *was to* do it at once. (*sollte = es war so vorgesehen, daß . . .*)

Put in shall, be to, or ought to / should.

a. I'm afraid I haven't got his address. But . . . . . I give you his phone number? b. If he's got a temperature, he . . . . . go straight to bed. c. . . . . . texts that treat Biblical stories as myths be allowed in textbooks? d. The marriage . . . . . take place next Saturday at 11 a.m. e. In Alf Garnett's opinion, mixed marriages . . . . . not be allowed. f. You say it doesn't work. . . . . . we exchange it for a new one then? g. The town fathers hired an energetic girl as a meter maid, who . . . . . patrol the streets checking the meters and issuing tickets to parking offenders. h. . . . . . I get you a bottle of beer from the fridge? – Yes, please. i. Every animal lover will agree that people like Mr Duffield . . . . . not be allowed to keep a dog. j. In his will, Mr Bates stipulated that his solicitor . . . . . select for his dog someone of proven good character, who had experience with animals. k. What do you want me to do? – . . . . . I ask them to reserve a table for us? l. I've just been told that I . . . . . be at the airport at three fifteen to meet Mr Stewart from Glasgow. m. You . . . . . not have missed the talk show on television last night. n. According to the will, the £4,160 legacy . . . . . be paid out at the rate of £10 a week for the next eight years to whoever gives the dog a good home. o. What . . . . . we do tonight? Have dinner at the Star of India?

13K **What oder which?** (→ GII15–16, GIII9)

What countries with more than one official language can you think of?
was für Länder?
Which part of Australia is the most densely populated?
welcher Teil Australiens?

What fragt allgemein, während *which* (aus einer beschränkten Auswahl) aussondert.

Put in what or which.

a. . . . . . similarities are there between songs and poems? b. . . . . . advice can you offer people who want to take unusual holidays? c. . . . . . cities will the President visit during his tour of Canada? d. . . . . . differences are there between England and Scotland? e. . . . . . floor do you live on? f. . . . . . German poet do you like best? g. In . . . . . respect is Quebec different from the rest of Canada? h. . . . . . kind of house do you live in? i. At . . . . . age do children finish primary school in this country? j. . . . . . rooms are there in your flat or house? k. So you have only three rooms. . . . . . room do you work in? l. Meet in January? Yes. . . . . . date do you suggest? m. . . . . . dogs' home did Mr Bates leave his money to?

13L **Passive. – Please complete.**

a. The dog . . . . . abandoned while its owner took a week's holiday at the seaside.
b. It was . . . . . without food or water during some of the hottest days of the year.
c. Mr Duffield was . . . . . for life from keeping a dog.
d. He was . . . . . £10 and ordered to pay £13 costs.
e. The dog . . . . . taken into care while a new home is sought for it.
f. Most dogs are . . . . . to death after a short, miserable existence.
g. For that reason, the breeding, selling, and keeping of dogs should . . . . . controlled more strictly.
h. Measures should be . . . . . to make it impossible for people like Mr Duffield to keep animals.

"When Flossie died, I decided not to get another cat."

13M **Ausdrücke mit Präpositionen**

as **as** a sign of my gratitude *als Zeichen meiner Dankbarkeit*	**on** the table **on** the right / left *die nebenstehende Tabelle*
at the assistant **at** Riley's *der Verkäufer bei Riley* **at** the seaside *an der See* a bottle of tomato ketchup **at** 34p *zum Preis von 34 Pence*	**over** **over** £4,000 *über 4000 Pfund* **such as** consumer magazines **such as** *Which?* *Verbraucherzeitschriften wie* Which?
by divide 80 **by** 16 *80 durch 16 teilen* **in** the best **in** the world *das beste (auf) der Welt* if you were **in** his position *wenn du an seiner Stelle wärest* what did he say **in** his defence? *was sagte er zu seiner Verteidigung?*	**to** the answer **to** a question *auf eine Frage* plead guilty **to** something *sich einer Sache schuldig bekennen* cruelty **to** animals *Grausamkeit gegenüber Tieren* cause suffering **to** someone *jemandem Leiden zufügen*
off a shop **off** Parliament Street *in einer Nebenstraße der P. Street*	**under** **under** this act *nach diesem Gesetz*

13N **Dictation exercise**

Two greyhounds that .... at London's .... Airport .... both very ill after .... flown from Ireland in .... that were .... small and .... ventilated, Uxbridge magistrates .... today.
One of the dogs was in a box shorter .... itself, and the other in a box .... made it .... for the dog to stand ...., it was ....
A dogs' home .... said both .... had grilles .... small for ventilation, and .... was blood around one grille .... the dog had .... to chew its way ....
An .... official .... the dogs had not .... carried in a way .... to .... them .... suffering and injury.

14L To-Infinitiv, -ing-Form oder Präposition + -ing-Form?

Change the following sentences as in the examples.

They had parking meters installed. (They decided . . .) They decided to have parking meters installed.
I wonder how he spent his school years. (I cannot help . . .) I cannot help wondering how he spent his school years.
He explained it to him. (He had no difficulty . . .) He had no difficulty in explaining it to him.

a. He always helps them. (He's always ready . . .) b. The Olympic Games open on 19 July. (The Olympic Games are due . . .) c. We heard that your flight was not very pleasant. (We were sorry . . .) d. At the moment he's planning his next trip. (. . . he's busy . . .) e. If you should require any further information, please let me know. (. . . please do not hesitate . . .) f. Will this advertisement attract suitable candidates? (Is this advertisement likely . . .) g. I meet lots of people. (I enjoy . . .) h. He never thinks about the future. (He refuses . . .) i. I learnt that poem at school. (I remember . . .) j. They found texts containing violence, sex scenes, and "gutter" language in the book. (They were disturbed . . .) k. The parking meters were anything but profitable. (The parking meters turned out . . .) l. She told them stories. (She went on . . .) m. The plans made by the architect were very difficult. (The plans made by the architect proved . . .) n. Then I bought the drinks. (Then it was my turn . . .) o. Would you answer me a few questions? (Would you mind . . .) p. He told me there was a lot of money to be saved by buying the jumbo size. (He had the cheek . . .) q. The flying time is very short. (The flying time seems . . .) r. Malta is an English-speaking country. (Malta has the advantage . . .) s. He met Mr Stewart during the second half of January. (He arranged . . .) t. I found out his name and address. (I managed . . .) u. They brought in a law against the killing of dogs for their skins. (They decided . . .) v. He did not accept them. (He always found reasons . . .) w. We'll see you on the 20th, then. (We'll look forward . . .) x. He caused unnecessary suffering to the dog. (He pleaded guilty . . .)

"What did you say you wouldn't mind doing?"

14M -ing-Konstruktion als adverbiale Bestimmung

Beachten Sie dieses wichtige Mittel zur Satzverkürzung (weitere Beispiele → GIV30–31):

Write a letter, **giving the required details and asking for further information about the club**.

Housing a concert hall with 2,700 seats, an opera hall with 1,550 seats and a small theatre, the Sydney Opera House is one of the most beautiful arts centres in the world.

Instead of going on wild spending sprees, he invested his money wisely.
You can save a lot of money **by buying the larger size**.

Please translate, using -ing constructions.

a. Ich schrieb diese Postkarte, während ich am Rand des Schwimmbeckens sonnenbadete. b. Er schrieb ihnen einen Brief, in dem er um weitere Einzelheiten bat. c. Der Junge verbringt eine Menge Zeit mit Fernsehen. d. Anstatt nach einem Krankenwagen zu telefonieren, trugen sie den alten Mann nach Hause. e. Er parkte seinen Wagen an einer Parkuhr, ohne eine Münze einzuwerfen. f. Nachdem er einige Sandwiches gegessen hatte, ging er hinauf auf sein Zimmer. g. Nachdem sie zwei Jahre bei ihren Eltern gewohnt hatte, mietete sie eine eigene Wohnung im Stadtzentrum. h. Da ich weiß, wie beschäftigt du bist, habe ich die Formulare für dich ausgefüllt. i. Da ich selber Mutter von vier (Kindern) bin, interessiere ich mich sehr für dieses Problem.

14N Saying the same thing differently

Ersetzen Sie die schräggedruckten Satzteile durch Formulierungen, die etwa dasselbe bedeuten.

a. *Are you keen on* adventure? b. Do you *enjoy travelling*? c. It's a job with *excellent* pay. d. What *kind* of work might *be involved*? e. Why don't you *join* our club? f. He wrote a letter, giving the *required* details. g. My spare-time activities *include* soccer, skin diving and travel. h. *At present* I am learning German at evening classes. i. I would be grateful if you could give *further* details about the job you are offering. j. If you should *require* any further information, please let me know. k. Experience would be useful but not *essential.*

140 **Infinitiv und -ing-Konstruktion in relativsatzähnlicher Funktion**
(→ GIII21 und GIII36)

Beachten Sie die folgenden wichtigen Möglichkeiten der Satzverkürzung:

England was the first country **to organize** a "Society for the Prevention of Cruelty to Animals".
(≈ . . . the first country that / which organized . . .)

The water **coming** from the tap was very hot.
(≈ The water that / which came . . .)

Change the following sentences as in the examples.

What are suitable souvenirs *that one might bring* home from Malta?
What are suitable souvenirs *to bring* homc from Malta?

The body was discovered by a neighbour *who looked* through the window of the flat.
The body was discovered by a neighbour *looking* through the window of the flat.

a. People who are thinking of suicide should phone The Samaritans.
b. They hired a girl who was to patrol the streets checking the meters.
c. He was unable to find anyone who could look after the dog.
d. We should all keep an eye on old people who live alone.
e. A document that says that you are permitted to drive a car is a driving licence.
f. An increasing number of youngsters who apply for work are hardly literate.
g. There are many historical sights that you can see.
h. The woman who showed me to my seat in the theatre told me that the gardener was the murderer.
i. Hand-made glass, gold and silver objects are the things you should look out for.
j. It's difficult for them to find a decent place where they could live.
k. The lessons that may be learnt from these stories can help the children in their own lives.
l. Most people are suspicious of reading material that reflects moral and political attitudes quite different from their own.
m. We require a salesman who will sell our products to shops in West Sussex.
n. Crime is one of the main problems that face the United States today.

14P **Satzverkürzung durch nachgestelltes Partizip Perfekt oder Adjektiv** (→ 6K)

> Which of the activities . . listed in the ad would you be interested in?
> Do these countries have separatist movements comparable to that in Quebec?

Please complete as in the examples.

a. I think he might be interested in the activities . . . . . by the club. b. TIME-OFF CLUB puts you in touch with intelligent people . . . . . in social activities. c. Could you draw up an advertisement . . . . . to attract candidates . . . . . for the job. d. I am interested in the job prospects . . . . . by you and would like to find out more about the type of work . . . . . e. There's an exciting job . . . . . in the *Evening News.* f. In a will . . . . . yesterday, Mr James Arthur Bates of 17 Willmore Drive, Poole, left over £4,000 to his dog, Fred. g. The pensioner . . . . . dead in his flat yesterday may have died months ago. h. Parents in the United States are becoming increasingly critical of the textbooks . . . . . in their children's schools. i. At the Green Banana Dennis Bryan met a pretty girl . . . . . Judy. j. A traffic warden has to check cars . . . . . at parking meters. k. The information . . . . . in the prospectus is not quite correct. l. There are a lot of American-made programmes . . . . . by the West German, Austrian, and Swiss networks. m. According to official estimates, fewer than half the crimes . . . . . in the U.S. are reported to the police.

14Q **Dictation exercise**

For .... years now I've .... a member of a rather .... kind of club. Time-Off Club, as it is ...., helps you to spend your .... time as .... as .... in the company of people .... are interested in the same .... that you are interested in. For those .... on sport, for ...., the club .... ball games, ... or mountain-.................... holidays, sailing or skin-diving .... If you .... just .... people ...., they offer you parties, ... out, dancing, ..., or .... things. If you are .... of travelling, you can .... your weekends visiting interesting places, sightseeing, ..., hiking, ..., or simply .... by the side of a hotel swimming pool. For members particularly .... on adventure, the club .... a trip .... across the Sahara last year. There's always something .... going on somewhere – Time-Off Club members never get ....

15 15M **Please complete.**

Patricia has . . . . . a prize in some sort of competition, ...?
Yes, she . . . . . A week's . . . . . for two in Ireland.
For two? So she can . . . . . someone along on the trip.
Yes, a . . . . . or relative or someone, whoever she . . . . .
. . . . . will they be travelling?
. . . . . train to London, and then . . . . . plane to Dublin.
But they won't be staying in Dublin all the time, ...?
No, of course not. They'll be . . . . . round Ireland in a luxury coach, and there'll be a guide who'll . . . . . everything to them.
And where will they . . . . . overnight?
At first-class hotels, in Killarney for . . . . ., and in Limerick.
That . . . . . really splendid. And it's all free?
Yes. They'll even be . . . . . seventy pounds spending money for the holiday.
Seventy pounds for each of . . . . .?
Well, I don't know. Maybe it's for the two of them . . . . . In . . . . . case, that's pretty generous, ...?
It certainly . . . . . When will she be . . . . . the holiday?
I've no idea. She can go . . . . . time . . . . . the end of May and the middle of September.

15N **At a bank** ꝏ

Can you give me Irish pounds for two hundred Deutschmarks / Swiss francs / Austrian schillings, please?
I'd like to change these marks (into pounds), please.
What's the rate (of exchange) for Deutschmarks? – About four to the pound.
Could you change this five-pound note for me, please? – How do you want it? – Pound notes and some coins, please.
Can I cash a Eurocheque here? / Do you accept Eurocheques? – Certainly. Would you please sign it and let me have your cheque card.

15O **At a post office** ꝏ

What's the postage on this letter to West Germany, please? – 19p, madam / sir. It's just over twenty grams. Here's the stamp. You can put the letter in the box over there.

15P **Complete the text, putting in the correct forms of words from the following list.**

become, buy, consist, cost, expect, form, invite, laugh, speak, state

Ireland is a republic . . . . . of 26 of the island's 32 counties – the other six . . . . . Northern Ireland, which is part of the United Kingdom. The Republic of Ireland . . . . . independent from Britain in 1921. The head of . . . . . is the President, but the leader of the government is the Prime Minister.
The languages . . . . . in Ireland are English and Irish.
A good restaurant meal . . . . . about £7 in Ireland.
If an Irishman . . . . . you to a pub, it is normal for him to . . . . . the first drink, after which you . . . . . the next, and so on. In company, each member of the party is . . . . . to buy "his" round of drinks.
In conversation, the Irish like to . . . . . at themselves and their institutions, but they don't like strangers to join in.

15Q **Dictation exercise**

Hören Sie das Diktat vom Tonband und schreiben Sie dabei diejenigen Wörter nieder, die im folgenden Diktattext fehlen.

Ireland is an ideal .... to spend a holiday. For .... who like the ...., there are 3,500 miles of .... with a lot of ...., uncrowded .... The .... with its ...., lakes, and countless .... and rivers is .... and largely .... the many .... attractions there are ...., cathedrals and other .... monuments as well as Ireland's .... customs and folklore. For .... keen on sports, there is tennis, ..., golf, riding and sailing; to the angler, Ireland offers some of .... finest fishing; for children there are .... holidays and many other ways to enjoy ....
If you are .... in a holiday in Ireland, write to the Irish .... Board in Dublin, asking for a copy of .... free .... brochure *Welcome to Ireland.*

15R Saying the same thing differently

Ersetzen Sie die schräggedruckten Satzteile durch Formulierungen, die etwa dasselbe bedeuten.

a. You will travel by *rail* to London and from there by *air* to Dublin. b. *A meal will be provided* on the train. c. You will then spend five days exploring some of the most beautiful *areas* of Ireland. d. You will *be provided with* £70 *spending* money for the holiday. e. *Departure from Peterborough would have to be* on a Sunday. f. Write a letter *in reply to* the above letter. g. She has just *come back* from her holiday in Ireland. h. Fuller details will be sent to you *shortly*. i. She *arrived* home *shortly* after ten o'clock.

15S Ausdrücke mit Präpositionen

among **among** our members *unter unseren Mitgliedern* they discussed it **among** themselves *sie diskutierten es untereinander*	**in** I'm interested **in** yoga *ich interessiere mich für Yoga* this results **in** earlier delivery *dies führt zu früherer Zustellung*
at **at** a banquet *bei einem Festessen* **at** present *im Augenblick*	**into** change marks **into** pounds *DM in Pfund umwechseln/umtauschen*
below the coupon **below** the advertisement *der Abschnitt unter der Anzeige*	**of** with the prospect **of** quick promotion *mit Aussicht auf schnelle Beförd.* 5 miles northwest **of** Cork *5 Meilen nordwestlich von Cork*
by send a letter **by** airmail *einen Brief per Luftpost schicken*	
for preparation **for** something *Vorbereitung auf etwas* ask **for** further information *um weitere Informationen bitten* apply **for** a place *sich um eine Stelle bewerben* look **for** something *etwas suchen*	**on** **on** the seventh day *am siebten Tag* **on** the west coast *an der Westküste* spend money **on** clothes *Geld für Kleidung ausgeben* are you keen **on** adventure? *sind Sie auf Abenteuer erpicht?*
	to welcome **to** Ireland! *willkommen in I.!*

15T **Listening comprehension** ⚭

Listen to the texts on tape and choose the right answer.

a. The traffic warden says
  1 you can only park at a parking meter for half an hour.
  2 you're lucky because normally you would have to pay a £6 fine.
  3 you've got to pay £6 to stop them towing your car away.
  4 they nearly towed the car away.

b. You want to buy tea in a tin, and are prepared to pay up to £1.75, so
  1 you choose the Indian Queen because it's cheapest.
  2 you don't buy the China tea because it's too expensive.
  3 you don't buy the Indian Queen because it's not in a tin.
  4 you don't buy the Twining's tea because of the packet.

c. They are looking for somebody
  1 who can do public-relations work in English and German.
  2 who has knowledge of Chicago or Stuttgart.
  3 who is interested in public-relations work but who needn't have experience in it.
  4 who speaks American English, not British English.

d. The travel agent says that
  1 the holiday begins in Rosslare.
  2 the price of the holiday includes petrol, but not lunch.
  3 you have to book the accommodation in advance after you've booked the package holiday.
  4 you stay 8 nights in 6 different towns.

e. The bank clerk says
  1 English pounds cannot be used in Scotland.
  2 she always uses up her Scottish notes before she goes to England.
  3 some people in England won't accept Scottish money.
  4 you should change your English pounds into Scottish ones before you enter Scotland.

We heard a loud noise in the room next to **our room**. We heard a loud noise in the room next to **ours**.
Big shops are not always cheaper than small **shops**. Big shops are not always cheaper than small **ones**.
Their English is improving, and **their job prospects are improving, too**. Their English is improving, and **so are their job prospects**.
Can he swim? – No, he **can't swim**. Can he swim? – No, he **can't**.
If you park your car longer than you are allowed **to park it**, the traffic warden will give you a ticket. If you park your car longer than you are allowed **to**, the traffic warden will give you a ticket.
There are many historical sights **which you must see**. There are many historical sights **to see**.
I was run into by a car **which was going** in the opposite direction. I was run into by a car **going** in the opposite direction.
You should always wear seat belts **when you are driving**. You should always wear seat belts **when driving**.
Since they were migrants with a poor knowledge of English, they could not find the kind of work they had been trained for. **Being migrants** with a poor knowledge of English, they could not find the kind of work they had been trained for.
The prize includes everything **that is described** below. The prize includes everything **described** below.
Thanks a lot for the fascinating little book **which you sent us** for Christmas. Thanks a lot for the fascinating little book **you sent us** for Christmas.

Change the following sentences as in the above examples.

a. Australians are beginning to accept people like us who have a background different from *their background.* b. She bought a jumbo packet and a few small *packets.* c. I work ninety hours a week, and *my wife works ninety hours a week, too.* d. I wouldn't help you even if I *could help you.* e. We'd like to join you, but I'm afraid we won't be able *to join you.* f. They had been unable to find anyone *who would have looked* after the dog while they were away. g. For companies *who advertise* on television it is profitable if the programmes contain as much sex and violence as possible. h. He should have fastened his seat belt *before he drove* away. i. *Since I am* a mother of four myself, I am very interested in this question. j. She won the second prize in a competition *which was run* by Holiday magazine. k. That was something *that you shouldn't have missed.* l. These tickets were rather expensive, but I couldn't get any cheaper *tickets.* m. I love the dog very much, and *Jack loves him very much, too.* n. Not all people feel the way you *feel* about dogs. o. *After he had studied* at Oxford, he became a clerk in the Patent Office. p. They could not find the kind of work *for which they had been trained.* q. *After I had eaten* a light supper, I went up to my room. r. What happens if you park your car at a meter *but don't put* a coin in? s. The future is something *about which he refuses to think.* t. In my last job I worked much less than I *work* now.

16L **Indirekte Rede** (→ GIV20)

"I wasn't wearing my seat belt." (He admitted . . .) He admitted (that) he hadn't been wearing his seat belt.

Change the following sentences as in the above example.

a. "I was on my way to work." (She said in her statement . . .)
b. "I didn't notice the other car following me." (The taxi driver said . . .)
c. "I've been driving for years and I've never had an accident." (She said . . .)
d. "Mr Bates left over £4,000 to his dog." (The neighbours were surprised to hear . . .)
e. "Where did you learn your excellent English?" (They asked him . . .)
f. "How did the accident happen?" (The policeman tried to find out . . .)
g. "What injuries did you receive in the accident?" (The insurance company wrote me a letter asking . . .)
h. "Did you check the oil?" (She asked the attendant . . .)
i. "Did you call the police?" (I was asked . . .)
j. "Did you buy the scarf at Selfridges?" (She asked Dick . . .)

16M At a garage / petrol station ꝏ

Six (gallons) of three-star, please.
Five pounds worth of regular / super, please.
Fill her up, please.
(Would you) Check the oil / tyres / battery, please.
Give me half a pint of oil, please.
Can you clean the windscreen, please.
Do you have a road map of this area?
Do you sell cigarettes / chocolates / biscuits / sweets / newspapers / paper handkerchiefs?

"Think of it this way – a gallon of our tea would cost you £2.50."

16N Deutsch: "man" – Englisch: Passiv

Man brachte ihn ins Krankenhaus.
He was taken to hospital.

Please translate, using the passive.

a. Man lud ihn zum Abendessen ein.
b. Wie hat man Sie im Lager (*camp*) behandelt?
c. Man hat meinen Wagen abgeschleppt.
d. Man zeigte ihr alle Sehenswürdigkeiten von Dublin.
e. Man schickte (*send – sent – sent*) ihm die kostenlose Broschüre *Willkommen in Irland.*
f. Hier spricht man Englisch.
g. Man sollte die Leute nicht zwingen, Sitzgurte zu tragen.
h. Die folgenden Einzelheiten sollte man sich notieren.
i. Man sollte das Züchten, Verkaufen und Halten von Hunden strenger kontrollieren.
j. Warum konnte man die Pläne nicht ändern?

"Careful, Wally, there's a drunk driver ahead!"

160 **Dictation exercise**

Hören Sie das Diktat vom Tonband und schreiben Sie dabei diejenigen Wörter nieder, die im folgenden Diktattext fehlen.

The experts tell us it's .... to .... seat belts when driving. Statistics ...., they say, that in most accidents you're much more likely not to get .... hurt if you're strapped to your seat and can't be thrown against the ...., the steering ...., or some other .... part of the car. Motorists often .... to think it would be safer for them to be thrown out of the car in the .... of an accident, but the statistics .... no .... that being thrown out more than .... the risk of being killed. An argument .... heard is that in the .... of the car .... fire, the people inside would be .... But .... to the experts, this argument doesn't .... water: fire is .... in less .... 1% of all accidents. And .... if the car does .... fire, people strapped to .... seats have a better chance of .... because the risk of .... being .... unconscious is much ....

"I don't think my dog wants me to take a breath test, officer."
(breath test ['breθ test] = Atemtest)

17G -ing-Form mit eigenem Sinnsubjekt (→ GIII35)

The boy is hanging around at home all the time. (We must prevent . . .) We must prevent the boy hanging around at home all the time.
He said something about it. (I remember . . .) I remember him saying something about it.

Change the following sentences as in the above examples.

a. Our customers do their shopping elsewhere. (We must prevent . . .)
b. A policeman was very kind to her when she was all dazed and shaken. (She said something about . . .)
c. A young woman was being beaten up by a man in the street. (I saw . . .)
d. He took up part-time work. (What reason did she give for . . .)
e. It is so small. (Why is Malta so attractive a place in spite of . . .)
f. They live in retirement towns like Worthing. (How can we prevent . . .)
g. They call him Piggy. (Doesn't he mind . . .)
h. We found a suitable hotel. (Everything now depended on . . .)
i. He's set up a business of his own. (What was his boss's reaction to . . .)
j. I mentioned his name. (Don't you remember . . .)
k. I live in a bungalow in Spain. (I can't imagine . . .)

17H Be supposed to = "sollen" (→ 13J, GV15)

Die Jüngeren sollen fixer und gescheiter sein.
The younger men are supposed to be quicker and brighter.

Please translate, using supposed to.

a. Es soll ein sehr hübscher Bungalow sein.
b. Worthing soll ein typisches "retirement centre" sein.
c. Dieses Buch von der Pre-Retirement Association soll viele wichtige Informationen enthalten.
d. Sitzgurte sollen am meisten bei Frontalzusammenstößen helfen.
e. Er soll nach Spanien gefahren sein.
f. Er soll gesagt haben, daß das Buch für Jugendliche ungeeignet sei.

17I Infinitiv oder -ing-Form nach Verb + Objekt

My father uses secondhand spectacles from a jumble sale. (I wouldn't want . . .) I wouldn't want my father to use secondhand spectacles from a jumble sale.
My father uses secondhand spectacles from a jumble sale. (I couldn't imagine . . .) I couldn't imagine my father using secondhand spectacles from a jumble sale.

Change the following sentences as in the above examples.

a. She wrote to a newspaper about her experience. (What caused . . .)
   She wrote to a newspaper about her experience. (What prevented . . .)
b. He took dancing lessons. (I encouraged . . .)
   He took dancing lessons. (She said something about . . .)
c. You checked the oil. (I remember . . .)
   You checked the oil. (I told . . .)
d. They keep a dog. (The landlord wouldn't allow . . .)
   They keep a dog. (The landlord wouldn't mind . . .)
e. She goes on holiday alone. (Fancy . . .)
   She goes on holiday alone. (I asked . . .)
f. We'll arrange accommodation. (Would you like . . .)
   We'll book a room for you at a hotel. (Would you mind . . .)
g. The injured animal was destroyed. (The policeman ordered . . .)
   The injured animal was destroyed. (The policeman prevented . . . from . . .)
h. I am against the project. (You're right about . . .)
   I am against the project. (They hadn't expected . . .)
i. The retirement age will be brought down from 65 to 60. (I'm against . . .)
   The retirement age will be brought down from 65 to 60. (I wouldn't like . . .)

17J Dictation exercise

.... of old people are living in .... in seaside towns to .... they have .... Pensioners who want to .... the rest of their .... in .... and .... often find heartbreak .... as inflation eats away their .... savings and they are left .... and forgotten. In Worthing, for ...., there are .... old people who never .... have a visitor. Worthing's medical and social .... just cannot .... with the demands of the .... old people who are now living in the ....

There have .... reports of old people never going out .... of untreated .... problems, and of pensioners .... someone .... dentures or glasses .... they cannot get National Health .... or .... they would be .... to pay .... bills.
There are similarly .... conditions in many other seaside ....
People .... from industrial .... to the .... dreaming of a happy retirement. But things are .... when they get there.
Experts on retirement problems give this ....: Stay at home where you .... when the time comes to give up your job. Prepare .... for retirement. Think of .... hobbies and other activities that will .... you meaningfully ....

17K **Ausdrücke mit Präpositionen**

Choose the correct answer.

a. What would you do if you were . . . . . my position?
   1. at 2. in 3. of 4. on
b. How nice to see you. Welcome . . . . . London!
   1. at 2. by 3. in 4. to
c. You should have sent the letter . . . . . airmail.
   1. by 2. in 3. per 4. with
d. Over half of all injuries to car users occur within a few miles . . . . . their homes.
   1. from 2. of 3. off 4. to
e. What are your views . . . . . this problem?
   1. in 2. on 3. over 4. to
f. He was brought to court . . . . . a charge of causing unnecessary suffering to a dog.
   1. by 2. on 3. under 4. with
g. I'm not against seat belts . . . . . principle.
   1. by 2. from 3. on 4. out of
h. Fortunately, I was strapped . . . . . my seat when the accident happened.
   1. at 2. by 3. on 4. to

18I **To-Infinitiv, -ing-Form oder Präposition + -ing-Form?**

He wanted **to work** in the canteen.
He didn't mind **working** in the canteen.
He looked forward **to working** in the canteen.

Please complete.

a. She admitted (be) late for work on several occasions. b. The room has the advantage (be) large and quiet. c. Her employer was understandably annoyed (be) left alone. d. At the moment I'm busy (write) letters and (fill) in forms. e. I've decided (retire) at the earliest possible date. f. She mentioned the difficulty (find) new work. g. I enjoy (sit) here when it's nice and warm. h. Please don't forget (bring) your passport along when you come tomorrow. i. She was so ill that she couldn't go on (work). j. She couldn't help (laugh) when she saw how embarrassed he was. k. Please do not hesitate (let) me know if there is anything else that I can do for you. l. What do you intend (do) after you've finished (study)? m. I'd be interested (hear) your opinion. n. To tell the truth, I don't particularly like (have) to work on Saturdays. o. He pleaded guilty (cause) unnecessary suffering to the dog. p. I would prefer (give) you an anaesthetic if you have nothing against it. q. I remember (see) him in Selfridges a few days ago. r. I'm sorry (hear) that you're still out of work. s. I'm thinking (give) up my job at the factory and (start) a business of my own.

18J **What did they actually say?**

He told Mrs Green that a holiday was out of the question for her.
"A holiday is out of the question for you, Mrs Green."

Change the following sentences into direct speech.

a. He warned her that if she took the holiday, she would be sacked. b. Mr Wood claimed that Mrs Green gave him only four days' notice that she intended to take the holiday. c. He said that the rule was for all the firm's employees to take their holidays at the same time. d. He explained that this year in particular, exceptions could not be made because of the difficult economic situation. e. Mrs Green claimed she told Mr Wood about the holiday two weeks before. f. She said her husband had arranged the holiday as a surprise for her and didn't tell her too soon because he knew how excited she got.

Julie (Wilkins) / Miss Wilkins She Mr Jackson Her boss / employer He The chairman of the (industrial) tribunal	(also)	said / declared / explained . . . told the tribunal . . . claimed . . . admitted . . . added . . . asked / wanted to know . . .

Change the following sentences into indirect speech, using phrases from the above table. Example:

"I took two days off from work without asking permission."
Julie admitted that she had taken two days off from work without asking permission.

a. "Mr Jackson dismissed me on the spot."
b. "Why did you stay away from work without asking permission?"
c. "My fiancé broke off our engagement three weeks before the wedding. I went on working until two days before the cancelled wedding but then felt I couldn't go on."
d. "Did you try to find another job, Miss Wilkins?"
e. "I've applied for 45 jobs since then – with no success. I'm quite sure my dismissal has been counting against me."
f. "Why did you dismiss Miss Wilkins without notice, Mr Jackson?"
g. "Apart from staying away without permission, Miss Wilkins was frequently late for work and used bad language on the phone."
h. "Is it true that you were late for work and used bad language on the phone, Miss Wilkins?"
i. "I was late because of poor bus services during the holiday period. I used strong language on one occasion when I was talking to my mother on the phone."
j. "None of the reasons given by the employer can justify instant dismissal. Miss Wilkins was given no chance to state her own case, and that's completely against the law."

18L To-Infinitiv nach for + Substantiv bzw. Pronomen (→ GIII27, 6O)

Es ist unbedingt notwendig, daß wir pünktlich sind. It is absolutely necessary for us to be punctual.

Please translate, using the for + object + infinitive construction.

a. Ist es wirklich notwendig, daß ich die Taschentücher bügle? b. Ist es in Ordnung, wenn ich diese Woche zwei Tage frei nehme? c. Es wäre verständlich, wenn er verärgert wäre. d. Es ist nicht normal, wenn ein Hund seinen eigenen Herrn beißt. e. Für eine Sekretärin ist es wichtig, daß sie adrett aussieht. f. Die Regel ist, daß alle Angestellten ihren Urlaub gleichzeitig nehmen. g. Es ist nicht warm genug, um die Klimaanlage einzuschalten.

18M Saying the same thing differently

Ersetzen Sie die schräggedruckten Satzteile durch Formulierungen, die etwa dasselbe bedeuten.

a. An industrial tribunal *is made up* of two people. b. When she *returned,* she was *dismissed.* c. When I *got back,* Mr Jackson just *wouldn't* listen. d. Julie's *boss* claimed that she had been late for work and used *bad* language on the phone. e. *Mr Jackson was understandably* annoyed at being left alone. f. *My back hurts.* g. A holiday is *out of the question* at this time of the year. h. She *gave her boss only four days' notice* that she *intended* to take the holiday. i. Mrs Green claimed she told Mr Wood about the holiday two weeks *before.* j. Other employees *were often allowed* to take their holidays at different times.

18N Dictation exercise

A 19-year-old dentist's .... who took two days .... because she was upset .... her wedding to a .... being .... off told an industrial tribunal in London yesterday that she was .... when she ....
Miss Julie Wilkins, of 4 Farm Street, W.1, was .... £390 for unfair ....
by Mr Kenneth Jackson, dental surgeon (= dentist), of 74 Harley Street, W.1.
Mr Jackson's ...., Miss Dorothy Young, said Mr Jackson told her to .... Miss Wilkins for being late, ... time .... without .... and .... strong .... on the phone.

 Listening comprehension ꝏ

Listen to the text on tape and decide whether the following statements are True (T) or Not True (NT).

(New words: discriminate against someone = jemanden diskriminieren; woodwork classes = [*etwa:*] Werkunterricht; needlework classes = [*etwa:*] Handarbeit.)

a. The speaker thinks the Government has still not done enough for women in spite of the new laws.
b. Women have had the same rights as men in all areas of society since 1970, at least on paper.
c. Some firms still do not treat women fairly.
d. The Equal Pay Act says that men and women doing the same work for different companies must get the same pay.
e. The Sex Discrimination Act is only about women's rights.
f. The Sex Discrimination Act deals with questions of equality in all areas except employment.
g. Landlords and school teachers are some of the people affected (= *betroffen*) by the Sex Discrimination Act.
h. Banks cannot offer a woman a different contract for a loan than a man if their financial situations are comparable.
i. The Sex Discrimination Act says a restaurant owner can no longer refuse to serve people because of their clothing, e.g. if a woman is not wearing a dress or a man is not wearing a suit.
j. If a man and a woman are both applying for a job and the man has only slightly better qualifications, many employers nowadays give the job to the woman because of the new act.
k. Advertisements asking for a waitress are illegal.
l. You often see funny-sounding advertisements for non-female secretaries in English papers nowadays.

19H Passiv

They treat him like a grown-up. – He is treated like a grown-up.
They found the children in different rooms. – The children were found in different rooms.

Change the following sentences into the passive. ꝏ

a. We expect our children to learn from us. b. Parents too often permit children to eat what they like. c. Somebody broke into our flat while we were away. d. Her boss gave her no chance to state her own case. e. They've made me organizer of the summer festival. f. Someone had heard a child calling from the flat. g. The firm had often allowed other employees to take their holidays at different times. h. We cannot make exceptions. i. I wouldn't consider this neighbourhood a very good place to grow up in. j. They will provide her with £70 spending money for the trip. k. I'll have to fill this tooth, I'm afraid.

19I Ausdrücke mit Präpositionen

Choose the correct answer.

a. Industrial tribunals deal ..... disputes between employees and employers.
   1. about 2. in 3. on 4. with
b. An industrial tribunal is made up ..... three people.
   1. by 2. from 3. of 4. with
c. I was talking to her ..... the phone the other day.
   1. at 2. by 3. on 4. through
d. During my last visit ..... London I suddenly got terrible toothache.
   1. at 2. in 3. of 4. to
e. She's a machinist ..... Polo Menswear Ltd.
   1. by 2. in 3. of 4. with
f. You have every right to be proud ..... what you've done.
   1. at 2. by 3. of 4. with
g. The children had been alone ..... fifteen hours.
   1. for 2. since 3. through 4. while
h. There was an interesting film ..... television last night.
   1. at 2. by 3. in 4. on

19J "Können" – "dürfen"

Please translate.

a. Auch der beste Fahrer kann in einen Unfall verwickelt werden.
b. Die Leute könnten denken, ich gebe ihm nicht genug Taschengeld.
c. Sie könnten jetzt von den Zinsen leben.
d. Sie konnten jetzt von den Zinsen leben.
e. Wie konnte sie mir das antun?
f. Das Kind hat Angst, daß jemand Böses in das Haus eindringen könnte.
g. Darf ich Sie einen Augenblick unterbrechen?
h. Als Kinder durften wir immer essen, was wir wollten.
i. Ich hatte ihm nicht helfen können.
j. Ich fürchte, wir werden nicht kommen können.

19K Dictation exercise

Hören Sie das Diktat vom Tonband und schreiben Sie dabei diejenigen Wörter nieder, die im folgenden Diktattext fehlen.

After .... 2,200 American children .... seven to eleven, experts have come to the .... that the kids feel .... good about ...., their parents, and their ....

.... to .... published ...., the .... majority of American children feel happy about their families and .... their parents are .... of them. .... two-thirds of the kids say their parents .... them "more like grown-ups" than "like a baby".
At the same time, ..., the children show an .... fear of the .... world. More than two-thirds .... that they are ".......... somebody bad .... get into the house", ... less than a third .... their own .... as "a very good place to .... up in".
At .... one in four .... that someone will .... him when he .... outside to play, and the same proportion say they are .... by .... programmes on television.

19L **Choose what you think is the most natural reply.**

a. Please pass on our very good wishes to Carol.
   1. I will do indeed. 2. I will that. 3. Yes, I do. 4. Yes, thanks.

b. Would you mind answering a few questions?
   1. No, I don't. 2. No, of course not. 3. Yes, I do. 4. Yes, of course.

c. Hello, Jack, how are you today?
   1. I'm fine, thanks. 2. Oh, I am, thanks. 3. Oh, thanks. 4. Thanks, I'm fine.

d. Thank you very much for your help.
   1. No thanks, sir. 2. Not at all, sir. 3. Oh, of course, sir. 4. Oh please, sir.

e. I hope you have a good journey.
   1. So I do. 2. So I have. 3. Thank you very much. 4. Yes, I will.

f. I love you, Alice.
   1. I as well, Archie. 2. I love you too, Archie. 3. I you too, Archie.
   4. So do I, Archie.

g. What's he like?
   1. He likes tea.
   2. He's ill.
   3. He's the architect.
   4. He's very nice.

h. Let me drive you home.
   1. It's a pleasure.
   2. Oh, indeed.
   3. Oh, that's very kind of you.
   4. Yes, I will.

i. What does he do?
   1. He does very well.
   2. He's a teacher.
   3. He's fine, thanks.
   4. He's on holiday.

j. I'd have liked to go.
   1. So did I.
   2. So had I.
   3. So have I.
   4. So would I.

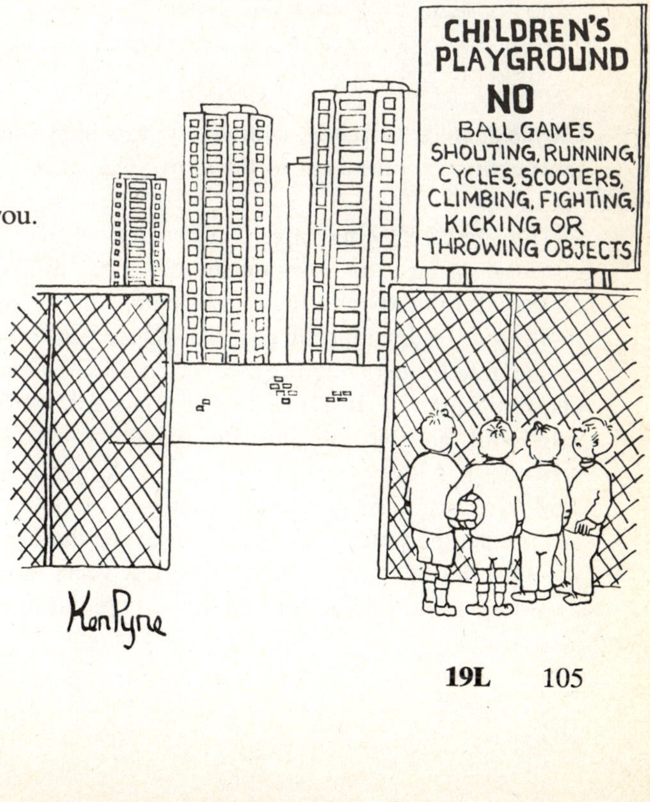

That was the laugh of the week. That **certainly** was the laugh of the week.
The policeman questioned her. The policeman (**really**) questioned her **thoroughly**.
I enjoyed the evening we spent together. I enjoyed the evening we spent together **very much**. I **very much** enjoyed the evening we spent together.
That's against the law. That's **completely** against the law.
The next day he was sick. The next day he was **terribly** sick.
A car park would be necessary. A car park would be **absolutely** / **really** necessary. A car park would **really** be necessary.
The situation is serious. The situation is **extremely** serious.
The problem you mentioned is a very serious one. The problem you mentioned is a very serious one **indeed**.

Use absolutely, certainly, completely, extremely, indeed, really, terribly, thoroughly, very much as in the above examples.

a. This increase in bus fares is necessary because of the rise in the cost of living. b. Music on buses is a wonderful idea. c. I dislike having to listen to that awful music. d. I find the music very relaxing. e. The music helps to drown the noise of the traffic. f. I should think it was dangerous for the driver to have music being blasted into his ears all the time. g. There's no need for him to have a loudspeaker near the front. h. If it was love at first sight, he didn't show it. i. Our holiday is wonderful, and we are enjoying ourselves. j. He was in high spirits when he arrived. k. I love you, Gwendolen. l. A man from the country would be lost in New York. m. I'm busy at the moment. n. Do you think there are people who can predict the future? o. We'd like to see the film. p. The film we saw last night was very boring. q. During the last few years the emergency medical service has been improved. r. She tried to lift him up, but it was impossible. s. In Australia, money is the only thing that counts. t. It's difficult for immigrants to find a job. u. The bus journey was very unpleasant. v. The pictures are splendid.

20J **Possessivpronomen oder Artikel?** (→ GIV13)

Put in: my, your, his, her, its, our, their, a(n), the.

a. If you see a parking meter with one of those "out of order" bags over . . . . . head, you can use it free of charge. b. If you're tired, you can just shut . . . . . eyes, lean back, and listen to the music. c. I helped him to . . . . . feet. d. His girl friend has been giving him . . . . . cold shoulder recently. e. This restaurant has lost much of . . . . . appeal since the new manager took over. f. The little girl put . . . . . arm through the iron grille of the shed. g. What would happen to the dog if . . . . . owner died? h. The driver has to keep . . . . . eye on things behind him in the bus. i. I have a little mole on . . . . . left shoulder and a small scar on . . . . . right knee. j. If the noise gets on . . . . . nerves, they can put ear plugs in . . . . . ears. k. At first we wanted to move to the south coast, but then we changed . . . . . minds. l. What is it that strikes you when you compare the size of Australia with the size of . . . . . population? m. The policeman shot him in . . . . . leg. n. If you do your work with . . . . . whole heart, you will succeed. o. The water was so hot that she scalded . . . . . hand.

20K **"Indem"**

> I tried to escape the music *by going downstairs.*
> Ich versuchte, der Musik zu entgehen, indem ich nach unten ging.

Translate the following "indem" sentences, using the by + -ing construction.

a. Sie brach ihren Arbeitsvertrag, indem sie ohne Erlaubnis Urlaub nahm.
b. Man kann viel Geld sparen, indem man die Jumbogröße kauft.
c. Die Omnibusgesellschaft versucht die Fahrpreise niedrig zu halten, indem sie ihre Dienstleistungen verringert.
d. Die Stadtväter lösten das Parkproblem, indem sie in der Innenstadt Parkuhren installieren ließen.
e. Er protestiert gegen die Fahrpreiserhöhung, indem er zu Fuß zur Arbeit geht.
f. Sie verbesserte ihr Englisch, indem sie ihren Sommerurlaub in England verbrachte.
g. Er sparte viel Zeit, indem er im Flughafenhotel übernachtete.

20L Saying the same thing differently

Ersetzen Sie die schräggedruckten Satzteile durch Formulierungen, die etwa dasselbe bedeuten.

a. The bus journeys are *bad* enough *nowadays, what with increased* fares and exact money *needed* on one-man buses. b. We *can really do without* the added agony of pop music. c. There was to be pop music *mixed* with *advertising* on the upper deck of some of Nottingham's buses. d. *No wonder* doctors' surgeries are *full of* people with nervous complaints. e. I think music on buses is *a wonderful* idea. f. I add my name to the long list of people who *hate* pop on buses. g. I have tried to *escape* the music by going downstairs. h. From the comments I have heard from other passengers, it seems to me that *the music is acceptable to the majority.* i. *Perhaps* the City Transport could *supply* cotton-wool ear plugs for *those* who cannot stand the music. j. There was a notice informing the public of another *increase* in bus fares. k. I don't *think the music on the buses is a* bad idea. l. *I suppose there's* something in that. m. *Anybody* who can't stand the noise *should* be *supplied* with free ear plugs.

20M Dictation exercise

The important question is not .... the kind of music .... on the buses is .... to passengers but .... we .... allow .... to do what they have never .... allowed to do before, that is, to .... advertising on .... who have no .... of .... it.
Advertising is .... annoying, but one can .... turn a radio or television .... or pay no attention to advertisements in the street or .... Against loudspeakers in a bus, ..., one is .... helpless.
The advertising .... is .... trying to get the public to .... something new and .... In a .... months we .... probably be told that the present ten minutes of advertising per .... is not profitable .... and that the proportion has to be .... Then one morning we .... find loudspeakers at bus stops so that we can have the .... of .... to pop and commercials .... we wait for the bus.
The time to stop this nonsense is now. .... must have the .... to travel on a bus in .... and ...., and the advertising .... and local .... must not be allowed to .... advertising on unwilling ...., and it .... not matter .... a majority of sixty-five or a .... of five per cent of the population are against advertising on buses.

Grammatikübersicht V GV

ABC einzelner Sprachgebrauchsprobleme

1 "Auch"

Bejahtes auch:
He speaks Spanish **too.**
He speaks Spanish **as well.**
He **also** speaks Spanish.
} *er spricht auch Spanisch*

Verneintes auch:
He doesn't speak Spanish **either**. *er spricht auch kein Spanisch*

She's **both** pretty **and** intelligent. *sie ist sowohl hübsch als auch intelligent*
She's **not only** pretty **but also** intelligent. *sie ist nicht nur hübsch, sondern auch intelligent*
She's pretty **as well as** intelligent.
She's pretty **and** intelligent **as well / too.**
} *sie ist hübsch und auch intelligent*

I'm staying at the Hilton. – **So am I.** *ich auch*
I haven't found a hotel yet. – **Nor / Neither have I.** *ich auch nicht*

2 "Brauchen"

You **needn't** help me.
You **don't need to** help me.
You **don't have to** help me.
} *Sie brauchen mir nicht zu helfen*

How many bottles will you **need**? *wie viele Flaschen werden Sie brauchen?*
I don't **need** the drill any more. *ich brauche den Bohrer nicht mehr*

It took him two hours to repair it.
He took two hours to repair it.
} *er brauchte zwei Stunden, um es zu reparieren*

Bruchzahlen

3 Gemeine Brüche

$\frac{1}{2}$ a half / one half	$\frac{3}{4}$ three quarters
$\frac{3}{2}$ three halves	$\frac{4}{5}$ four fifths
$\frac{1}{3}$ a third / one third	$1\frac{1}{2}$ one and a half
$\frac{2}{3}$ two thirds	$2\frac{1}{3}$ two and a third
$\frac{1}{4}$ a quarter / one quarter	$4\frac{3}{4}$ four and three quarters

$\frac{1}{2}$ lb butter = half a pound / *US* a half pound of butter
$\frac{1}{4}$ mile = a quarter of a mile
$\frac{5}{8}''$ = five eighths of an inch
$1\frac{3}{4}''$ = one and three-quarter inches / an inch and three quarters
$\frac{145}{360}$ = 145 over 360

He spent **half an hour** / *US* **a half hour** at her bedside. *eine halbe Stunde*
The buses run **every half hour**. *die Busse verkehren alle halbe Stunde*
They sold it **(at) half price**. *zum halben Preis*
Half of 52 is 26. *die Hälfte von 52 ist 26*
She bought **half a cake**. *sie kaufte einen halben Kuchen*
She bought **a quarter (of a pound)** of butter. *ein Viertelpfund Butter*
He received **one third** / **a third of the money**. *ein Drittel des Geldes*

4 Dezimalbrüche

0.56 nought [nɔ:t] point five six *0,56 null Komma fünf sechs*
5.40 five point four nought / oh *5,40 fünf Komma vier null*

a. Der Dezimalpunkt steht im britischen Englisch häufig auf halber Höhe: 0·56, 5·40.
b. Statt *nought* / *oh* wird im amerikanischen Englisch *zero* ['zɪərəʊ] gelesen.
c. Bei Dezimalbrüchen unter 1 wird die Null vor dem Dezimalpunkt mitunter weggelassen: .56 / ·56 (point five six).

5 Datum

July 16, 1979	July 16th, 1979
16 July, 1979	16th July, 1979
16 July 1979	16th July 1979

July (the) sixteenth, nineteen (hundred and) seventy-nine
the sixteenth (of) July, nineteen (hundred and) seventy-nine

6 "Dürfen"

May I ask you some questions? – Yes, you **may**. / No, you **may** not. *darf ich . . .? – ja, Sie dürfen / nein, Sie dürfen nicht*
You **mustn't** take these things so seriously. *du darfst . . . nicht*
That **can't** be true! *das darf doch nicht wahr sein!*
He **wasn't allowed to** leave the house. *er durfte . . . nicht verlassen*
Smoking **is not allowed** here. *hier darf nicht geraucht werden*
The dog **isn't allowed** (to come) in. *der Hund darf nicht herein(kommen)*
He **ought to** / **should** be back by now. *er dürfte inzwischen zurück sein*
You **shouldn't** have done that. *das hättest du nicht tun dürfen*

7 "Es"

The child is sleeping, don't wake **him** / **her** up. *wecke es nicht auf!*
He isn't likely to come. *es ist nicht wahrscheinlich, daß er kommt*
I'm glad to see you. *es freut mich, dich zu sehen*
I'm surprised he didn't come. *es wundert mich, daß er nicht gekommen ist*

Is that you, Stephen? *bist du es, Stephen?*
It's me. *ich bin's*
Is there a similar title in German? *gibt es einen ähnlichen Titel im Deutschen?*
There was a quarrel, and the architect resigned. *es gab Streit*
There was a lot of dancing. *es wurde viel getanzt*

8 "Kein"

We do**n't** have **any** tomatoes. *wir haben keine Tomaten*
She has**n't** got **a** room of her own. *sie hat kein eigenes Zimmer*

He is**n't a** good singer. *er ist kein guter Sänger*
He's **not much of a** gardener. *er ist kein großer Gärtner*

Nobody / No one can help me. *mir kann keiner helfen*
None of you can help me. *keiner von euch kann mir helfen*

I do**n't** know **anybody / anyone** who plays as well as he does. *keinen, der so gut wie er spielt*
I do**n't** know **any** of his friends. *ich kenne keinen seiner Freunde*

9 "Können"

Can you help me? *können Sie mir helfen?*
The boy **cannot** swim yet. *der Junge kann noch nicht schwimmen*
Can she speak / Does she know any English? *kann sie Englisch?*
I won't **be able to** come. *ich werde nicht kommen können*
They **may** arrive (at) any moment. *sie können jeden Augenblick ankommen*
She **might** have known that we were worried. *sie hätte sich ja denken können, daß wir uns Sorgen machen*

10 "Lassen"

Leave me alone for a while, please. *laß mich . . . in Frieden!*
Why did you **leave** the door open? *warum hast du die Tür offengelassen?*
You can **leave** the lights on. *du kannst die Lampen brennen lassen*
Her father doesn't **allow** her **to** go out so late. *läßt sie so spät nicht weggehen*
The doctor won't **allow** him **to** get up. *wird / will ihn nicht aufstehen lassen*
He **had** the letter **translated**. *er ließ den Brief übersetzen*
They **had** their breakfast **brought** up to their room. *ließen sich . . . aufs Zimmer bringen*
He **made** me feel that he was the boss. *er ließ mich fühlen, daß er der Chef war*

11 Much / many – a lot of ("viel / viele")

He has **a lot of** money in the bank. *er hat viel Geld auf der Bank*
He hasn't got **much** money in the bank. *er hat nicht viel Geld auf der Bank*
How **much** money have we got in the bank? *wieviel Geld haben wir auf der Bank?*

There were **a lot of** people at the meeting. *es waren viele Leute auf der Versammlung*
There weren't **many** people at the meeting. *es waren nicht viele Leute auf der Versammlung*
How **many** people were there at the meeting? *wie viele Leute waren auf der Versammlung?*

He gave us as **much** / **many** as he could. *er gab uns soviel / so viele, wie er konnte*
There's too **much** crime. There are too **many** meetings.
We saw so **much** misery / so **many** miserable people.

Much und *many* stehen überwiegend in verneinten Sätzen und Fragesätzen. In bejahten Sätzen kommen *much* und *many* vor allem nach *as, too* und *so* vor. Ansonsten ist es sicherer, in bejahten Sätzen anstelle von *much / many* einen Ausdruck wie *a lot of* zu gebrauchen.

12 "Müssen"

You **must** organize your work better. *du mußt deine Arbeit besser organisieren*
It **must** have been raining. *es muß geregnet haben*
The windows **have to** be kept closed in winter. *die Fenster müssen im Winter geschlossen bleiben*
You can pay in advance, but you don't **have to**. *aber Sie müssen es nicht*
You **ought to** / **should** have known that. *das hättest du wissen müssen*
I **couldn't help** laughing. *ich mußte einfach lachen*

13 "Sehr"

a. She is **very** happy. *sie ist sehr glücklich*
b. The music was **very** relaxing. *die Musik war sehr entspannend*
c. They were **very** tired. *sie waren sehr müde*
d. She speaks English **very** well. *sie spricht sehr gut Englisch*

---

e. I love her **very much**. *ich liebe sie sehr*
f. He liked the chicken curry so **much** that he asked the waiter for the recipe.
g. I **very much** enjoyed the evening we spent together. *ich habe den Abend . . . sehr genossen*
h. We miss him **very much**. *wir entbehren ihn sehr / er fehlt uns sehr*

Very ist in der Bedeutung "sehr" auf den Gebrauch bei Adjektiven (a–c) und Adverbien (d) beschränkt. Bei Verben steht nicht *very,* sondern *much* oder *very much* (e–h).

14 "Sich"

They bought **each other / one another** presents.	*sie kauften sich (= einander) Geschenke*
They bought **themselves** warm clothes.	*sie kauften sich (= für sich selbst) warme Kleidung*
They looked at **each other** / at **one another**.	*sie schauten sich (= einander) an*
They looked at **themselves**.	*sie schauten sich (= sich selbst, etwa im Spiegel) an*

15 "Sollen"

I **was to** spend the night at a hotel near the airport.
ich sollte in einem Hotel in der Nähe des Flughafens übernachten (das war so vorgesehen)
How **am** I **(supposed) to** solve that problem? *wie soll ich dieses Problem lösen?*
Am I **supposed to** eat all that? *soll ich das alles essen?*
He **is supposed / is said to** have known nothing about it. *er soll nichts davon gewußt haben*
Tell him **to wait**. *sag ihm, er soll warten*
Shall I wait here? / **Do you want me to** wait here? *soll ich hier warten?*
You **ought to / should** be thankful for what you have. *du solltest dankbar sein für . . .*

16 This – that

Grundsätzlicher Unterschied: *This / these* bezeichnet das örtlich, zeitlich oder gedanklich näher Liegende; *that / those* bezeichnet das örtlich, zeitlich oder gedanklich ferner Liegende.

This is an Alsatian, and **that** is a Labrador.	*dies ist ein Schäferhund, und das da ist . . .*
These are horses, and **those** are ponies.	*dies sind Pferde, und das da sind Ponys*
I like **this** country.	*(d. h.: das Land, in dem ich mich gerade befinde)*
I didn't like **that** country.	*(d. h.: ein anderes Land als das, in dem ich mich gerade befinde)*
I didn't see him **this** morning.	*heute morgen*
I didn't see him **that** morning.	*an jenem Morgen*
We're seeing a lot of each other **these** days.	*in diesen Tagen*
Houses were much cheaper in **those** days.	*in jenen Tagen / damals*
I can't stand **this** noise.	*ich kann diesen Lärm nicht vertragen*
What was **that** noise?	*was war das für ein Geräusch?*

17 "Werden"

He **became** an architect. *er wurde Architekt*
He's **going to be** an architect. *er wird Architekt / will Architekt werden*
Eggs have **become** very expensive. *Eier sind sehr teuer geworden*
She **was / got** bitten by an Alsatian. *sie wurde von einem Schäferhund gebissen*
She **got** very ill and had to be taken to hospital. *sie wurde sehr krank*
I suppose I'm **getting** older too. *ich werde wohl auch älter*

21H **Verstärkung durch do** (→ GII41)

We look forward to having you here. *wir freuen uns*
We **do** look forward to having you here. *wir freuen uns wirklich*

I said I'd phone you, and I phoned you. *habe dich angerufen*
I said I'd phone you, and I **did** phone you. *habe dich auch wirklich angerufen*

Use do / does / did as in the above examples.

a. We hope that you will both be able to come. b. I understand your difficulties. c. He said he would escape, and he escaped. d. I thought they would never finish it, but they finished it in the end. e. It sounds strange, doesn't it? f. The book contains a lot of violence, sex, and strong language. g. I like the new opera house. h. I admit that I had a very lazy youth. i. The music here gets on my nerves. j. They said they wouldn't raise fares, but they raised them in the end. k. Believe me: seat belts make driving safer. l. A car costs a lot of money, doesn't it? m. Stop that noise! n. Be serious for a moment!

21I **Verstärkung durch -self-Pronomen** (→ GIV15)

I'm a mother of four. *ich bin Mutter von vier Kindern*
I'm a mother of four **myself**. *ich bin selber Mutter von vier Kindern*

The house is very pleasant. *das Haus ist . . .*
The house **itself** is very pleasant. *das Haus selber ist . . .*

A trap, with me as the bait? *eine Falle, mit mir als Köder?*
A trap, with **myself** as the bait? *eine Falle, mit mir selbst als Köder?*

Use the -self pronouns as in the above examples.

a. I'm puzzled. b. What do you think of it? c. Why not tell Inspector Raglan? d. Have you ever been there? e. Her mother educated her. f. Some young people find the crimes on television so interesting that they try them out. g. The music is not too bad. h. I was pretty badly injured. i. I spoke to the murderer. j. Our neighbours' children are a noisy lot, but they are very quiet people. k. We always wear seat belts when driving. l. There are prizes for the winning secretary and for her boss. m. There are prizes for her and her boss. n. These tickets here are for the children, and these are for us.

21 J **Relativsätze** (→ GIV16, 11M)

Complete the following sentences, leaving the relative pronoun out where possible.

a. Police and firemen yesterday broke into a Birmingham flat from . . . . . a child had been heard calling. b. The first book . . . . . Agatha Christie wrote was turned down by six publishers before a seventh published it in 1920. c. I got only 80 per cent of the amount . . . . . was really due to me. d. The children were found in separate bedrooms, the doors of . . . . . were locked. e. The man . . . . . murdered Roger Ackroyd is in this room now. f. There are many old people . . . . . only friend and companion is a dog. g. The play . . . . . we saw last night has been running for about three years now. h. People . . . . . want to keep a dog should meet certain minimum requirements. i. I am unmarried and have no commitments . . . . . would keep me in this area. j. Can you suggest ways in . . . . . this problem might be overcome? k. Is she the woman . . . . . husband died in an accident some time ago? l. According to Agatha Christie, an archaeologist is the best husband . . . . . any woman can have. m. In 1930 Agatha Christie married an archaeologist, ... she later accompanied on many of his expeditions. n. Frank Harris, ... most of you will know, had a nasty accident this morning.

21 K **Hochleistungswort to**

Prägen Sie sich die folgenden Ausdrücke mit *to* ein.

complain **to** somebody *sich bei jem. beschweren*
take a fancy **to** somebody *an jem. Gefallen finden*
treat somebody **to** champagne *jem. zu Champagner einladen*
leave money **to** somebody *jem. Geld hinterlassen*
bring somebody **to** court *jem. vor Gericht bringen*
put an animal **to** death *ein Tier zu Tode bringen / töten*
cause unnecessary suffering **to** a dog *einem Hund unnötiges Leiden zufügen*
cruelty **to** animals *Grausamkeit gegenüber Tieren / Tierquälerei*
the tickets will be sent **to** you shortly *die Karten werden Ihnen in Kürze zugesandt*
in reply **to** your letter *in Beantwortung Ihres Schreibens*
plead guilty **to** something *sich einer Sache schuldig bekennen*
the amount that was due **to** me *der Betrag, der mir zustand*

21L "Werden" (→ GV17)

Translate the following sentences, using become, get, or be to express "werden".

a. *The Murder of Roger Ackroyd* ist einer der berühmtesten Kriminalromane aller Zeiten geworden.
b. Je älter sie wird, desto attraktiver wird sie.
c. Wenn er auf die Universität gegangen wäre, wäre er vielleicht Archäologe geworden.
d. Dein Essen wird kalt, Jack.
e. Um diese Jahreszeit wird es früh dunkel.
f. Hoffentlich wirst du bald wieder gesund.
g. Ich würde krank (werden), wenn ich in diesem Haus wohnen müßte.
h. So etwas sollte nicht erlaubt werden.
i. Sie wurde von ihrer Mutter unterrichtet und konnte schon mit vier Jahren lesen.
j. Ihr erstes Buch wurde von sechs Verlegern abgelehnt, bevor ein siebenter es 1920 herausbrachte.
k. Dieser Film wird seit Anfang Januar gezeigt.

21M Dictation exercise

Hören Sie das Diktat vom Tonband und schreiben Sie dabei diejenigen Wörter nieder, die im folgenden Diktattext fehlen.

Sir Max Mallowan, one of the .... British archaeologists, ... on August 19, 1978, ... seventy-four. Mallowan's first .... was Agatha Christie, one of the .... most .... and .... of detective ....
He met her .... an expedition to Iraq and .... her in 1930.
Agatha Christie .... her husband on many of his expeditions and took a .... interest in his .... work. The .... lasted over .... years .... Agatha Christie .... at the .... of 1976.
In 1977, Mallowan .... a second time, this time a .... archaeologist.
Mallowan was the author of .... important .... works.
His spare-time interests .... gardens, ..., English ...., and ....

21 N **Listening comprehension** ꝏ

In each of the following five questions you will hear one person speaking. Listen to what the person says, then read the question, then listen again and decide which answer is correct.

a. What does the policeman want you to do?
   1 Be ready to make a written statement later if required.
   2 Go to the police station with him.
   3 Just give him your name and address so that he can contact you later.
   4 Make a written statement now.

b. What did the spokesman say?
   1 Fares had been increased three times already in the last 18 months.
   2 Fares were going up because of improved services.
   3 More money for the workers was part of the reason for the change.
   4 Operating costs had risen by more than 8% in the past few months.

c. You are free on the four following days and are prepared to spend up to £6.50. When do you decide to go?
   1 Monday
   2 Saturday
   3 Thursday
   4 Tuesday

d. You want to get to Wendover.
   1 You can get there if you change at Amersham.
   2 You can get there if you change at Aylesbury.
   3 You can't get to Wendover direct at all today.
   4 You have no choice. You must wait till 11.15.

e. Your toothache is very painful.
   1 Mr Webb's receptionist will arrange an appointment with Mr Stockton or Mrs Beales.
   2 The best thing to do is to go to Mr Webb's surgery.
   3 The hospital is the only place you can get help.
   4 You can ring for an appointment at Mrs Beales' and Mr Stockton's surgery.

22G **Ask questions as in the examples.**

Linda Brown had to go to *an all-black* school. *What (kind of)* school did Linda Brown have to go to?
I'm looking for a book *about haunted houses in London.* *What kind of* book are you looking for?

a. America's blacks fought for *equal* rights *in housing and employment, in recreation facilities and at the ballot box.* b. Many children are frightened by *violent* TV programmes. c. Councillor Morris is chairman of *the Social Services* committee. d. Parents are suspicious of reading material *reflecting moral and political attitudes quite different from their own.* e. The assistant recommended *an automatic* toaster. f. I'm interested in *18th-century English* books. g. We stayed at *a pleasant* hotel *by the seaside.* h. The average American adult wants *a child's* figure. i. He had *a very happy* youth. j. She died at *the* age *of 85.*

"Miss Ross! Would you tell me what time, date and month it is – my watch (Uhr) *has stopped."*

22H **Ask questions as in the examples.**

Twelve per cent of the U.S. population are blacks. *What percentage* of the U.S. population are blacks?
They flew by *British Airways.* *What airline* did they fly by?

a. They'll come *at five o'clock.*
b. They suggested *the 5th of January.*
c. He works for *Boyd & Company.*
d. He took A levels in *Economics and Maths.*
e. She wrote *detective novels.*
f. She'*s a dentist's receptionist.*
g. The first book she wrote *was turned down by six publishers.*

22I Do or make?

Put in the correct form of do or make.

a. Although great progress has been . . . . ., a lot remains to be . . . . . b. The boy doesn't even have a table to . . . . . his homework on. c. The detective who solved this murder case certainly . . . . . a good job. d. What do you . . . . . for a living, Mr Jackson? e. If you go to Portland, you should . . . . . an excursion to the White Mountains. f. Have you already . . . . . plans for your next holiday? g. We've been . . . . . business with Stewart & Son for many years. h. If their parents' marriage is unhappy, children are more likely to have health problems, ... poorly at school and have accidents. i. Do you think this book is suitable for being . . . . . into a film? j. My wife . . . . . the housework, and my son . . . . . the deliveries. k. He thanked her for . . . . . the tea. l. What shall we . . . . . tonight? Watch television, or have a drink at the White Horse? m. Her husband . . . . . most of the minor repairs himself. n. You should have . . . . . an appointment instead of just going straight there.

22J Infinitiv als Subjekt und Prädikativum

To be black usually means **to be** poor.
To live anywhere in the world today and be against equality is like living in Alaska and being against snow.
The best way to travel is **to walk.**

Please translate, using the infinitive as in the above examples.

a. Ein Auto zu besitzen heißt frei zu sein.
b. Für ihn zu kochen muß ein Vergnügen sein.
c. Ein Tier auszusetzen ist grausam.
d. Das Schlimmste, was man einem Hund antun kann, ist ihn auszusetzen.
e. Meine Aufgabe ist es, Münzen in alle Parkuhren zu stecken, die dabei sind abzulaufen.
f. Unser größtes Problem war eine geeignete Wohnung zu finden.
g. Siebzig Jahre jung zu sein ist besser als vierzig Jahre alt zu sein.
h. Sein oder Nichtsein, das ist die Frage.

22K **Hochleistungswort in**

the rise **in** the cost of living *der Anstieg der Lebenshaltungskosten*
another increase **in** fares *eine weitere Fahrpreiserhöhung*
what did he say **in** his defence? *was sagte er zu seiner Verteidigung?*
if I were **in** his place *wenn ich an seiner Stelle wäre*
give evidence **in** court *vor Gericht aussagen*
arguments **in** favour of seat belts *Argumente (, die) für Sitzgurte (sprechen)*
he's **in** love with her *er ist in sie verliebt*
fall **in** love with somebody *sich in jem. verlieben*
this car **in** particular *insbesondere dieses Auto*
in reply to your letter *in Beantwortung Ihres Schreibens*
in spite of the weather *trotz des Wetters*
in the long run *auf die Dauer / auf lange Sicht*
get to the airport **in** time *rechtzeitig zum Flughafen gelangen*
there's something **in** that *da ist was (Richtiges) dran*
this will result **in** earlier delivery *dies wird zu einer früheren Zustellung führen*

22L **Dictation exercise**

.... 1930 and 1975 the black population in the U. S. .... from 9.69 to .... per cent, and it is still ....

For someone looking at U. S. social .... it is .... to see that blacks are an .... minority. In 1976, the unemployment rate for .... people was .... that for whites. The unemployment problem was .... serious .... young non-white workers: over 37 per cent of non-whites under twenty .... out of work.

Looking at the distribution of personal incomes one .... that non-whites outnumber whites by three to one in the .... income .... (under $3,000), while top incomes ($25,000 and over) are .... earned by whites.

The number of U. S. cities .... by black .... has been .... in .... years. The main .... for this .... is that blacks have .... moved into the city centres while whites have moved out into the .... the .... of people now living in the inner cities are not only black but also poor, ... have their hands full .... to fight unemployment, crime, and the .... of slums.

23G Singular oder Plural?

a. The Government **have** decided . . . *die Regierung hat beschlossen*
b. The Government **was** embarrassed. *die Regierung war in Verlegenheit*

"Kollektivwörter" wie *government* (aber auch z. B. *opposition, family, public*) können als Singular (oben b) oder als Plural (oben a) konstruiert werden, je nachdem, ob man mehr an die Gesamtheit (b) oder die Mitglieder der Gruppe als einzelne (a) denkt.

Decide if one of the two forms is more natural, or whether both forms are equally natural.

a. The bus company . . . . . a duty to break even.
   1. has 2. have
b. The public . . . . . understandably annoyed at the fare increase.
   1. are 2. is
c. I have no idea how the tribunal . . . . . going to decide the case.
   1. are 2. is
d. The industrial tribunal . . . . . made up of three people.
   1. was 2. were
e. One-third of Worthing's population . . . . . aged over 65.
   1. are 2. is
f. The majority . . . . . in favour of the new law.
   1. are 2. is
g. The majority of motorists . . . . . not use seat belts.
   1. do 2. does

23H Singular or plural? Please translate.

a. Die Opposition versucht, den Wohlfahrtsstaat kaputtzumachen.
b. Eine neue Gruppe von Touristen ist gerade angekommen.
c. Der Sozialausschuß wird dieses Problem nächste Woche diskutieren.
d. Die Öffentlichkeit ist nicht bereit, eine weitere Fahrpreiserhöhung hinzunehmen.
e. Die Regierung erwägt eine Steuererhöhung.
f. Seine Familie freute sich sehr, diese Nachricht zu hören.

Beachten Sie:
He is married **to** an actress.
He is married **with** one child.
er ist verheiratet und hat ein Kind

231 **Some – any** (→ 12G)

Any workers without a job who decide to go on holiday to Spain will get full unemployment pay all the time they are there.
An archaeologist is the best husband **any** woman can have: the older she gets, the more interested he is in her.
Anybody who can't stand the noise should be supplied with free ear plugs.

Beachten Sie die obigen, von der in 12G gegebenen Regel nicht abgedeckten Beispiele. Hier stehen *any* und seine Zusammensetzungen im bejahten Satz in Bedeutungen wie "jede(r, s), ganz gleich welche(r, s)", "irgendein(e), ganz gleich welche(r, s)", "alle, ganz gleich welche", "alles, ganz gleich was" usw.

Put in some / any, somebody / anybody, someone / anyone, something / anything.

a. Agatha Christie made more money out of murder than . . . . . woman since Lucrezia Borgia. b. . . . . . has just told me that my car was towed away by the police. c. We will do . . . . . we can to help you. d. The Government should do . . . . . about it. e. When a dog bites . . . . ., it's often the humans who're at fault. f. Our dog has never bitten . . . . . g. People who are in despair can ring The Samaritans at . . . . . time of the day or night. h. I would be absolutely furious if this was allowed to happen to . . . . . of my children. i. The boy has probably picked up . . . . . infection. j. An adult burglar has only one chance in 412 of going to jail for . . . . . single burglary. k. She said she'd left the baby alone because she'd been unable to find . . . . . to look after it. l. It was not until the beginning of the 19th century that . . . . . measures were taken for the prevention of cruelty to animals. m. Can you take this call, Miss Hopkins? . . . . . customer of ours is complaining about our product.

"On holiday or dole?"

23J **Must not = darf nicht** (→ GV6)

The holiday **must not** / **mustn't** ['mʌsnt] last longer than one year.
der Urlaub darf nicht länger als ein Jahr dauern

In verneinender Antwort auf eine *may*-Frage ist "darf nicht" allerdings *may not*: *May I smoke here? – No, you may not.*

Please translate.

a. Sie dürfen nicht die Tatsachen verdrehen. b. Ich darf mich nicht beklagen. c. Wir dürfen den Mörder nicht entkommen lassen. d. Du darfst das Kind nicht erschrecken. e. Ein Gericht darf die Tötung eines Tieres anordnen, wenn es grausam wäre, es am Leben zu halten. f. Bis in die fünfziger Jahre durften schwarze Kinder keine weißen Schulen besuchen. g. Das dürfte der Briefträger sein. h. Das hätte nicht passieren dürfen.

23K **Hochleistungswort at**

he met her **at** a dance *er lernte sie auf / bei einer Tanzveranstaltung kennen*
he does poorly **at** school *er kommt in der Schule nicht gut mit*
they learn English **at** evening classes *sie lernen Englisch an / in der Abendschule*
they met **at** the appointed time *sie trafen sich zur verabredeten Zeit*
buy something **at** a discount *etwas verbilligt (ein)kaufen*
get up **at** sunrise *bei Sonnenaufgang aufstehen*
at night *am Abend / in der Nacht*
love **at** first sight *Liebe auf den ersten Blick*
the sum is to be paid out **at** the rate of £10 a week
die Summe soll in wöchentlichen Raten von 10 Pfund ausgezahlt werden
at a pinch you could sleep on the couch *zur Not / notfalls könntest du auf der Couch schlafen*

23L **Dictation exercise** ꝏ

Fred O'Neill has not had a job for seven .... He was .... out of work at the .... of 32, and unless something very .... happens, he is not

.... ever to work again. Every .... he .... his "wages", as he calls them, from a Government office; every .... his wife .... the family allowance from another Government office; every week they and .... five children are as .... as .... with the ...., hoping that there .... be any unexpected ....

The O'Neills live in a .... house in a small industrial town in Cumbria, where the .... rate is three times the national .... There are jobs at the local labour ...., but for Fred O'Neill they are .... of the .... sort or in the .... place. He .... to accept a job at less .... he gets on the dole because of the children.

After .... school, Fred had worked as a labourer for 16 .... until .... ulcers .... him to look for lighter work. He joined a Government .... to be .... as a lathe operator and .... quickly .... a job. For the first, and .... only, time in his life he was .... good wages. .... three months, as a result of the .... financial ...., he .... himself on the dole.

"Excuse me, sonny, this is a bench for the retired – the unemployeds' benches are on the other side."

New words in this text:

unless = if . . . not

family allowance = (in Britain) a sum of money paid weekly to every family for each child

bench = a long seat (as in a park) for two or more people to sit on

24H **Indirekte Rede** (→ GIV20)

> "He'll never get planning permission." (People said . . .)
> People said (that) he'd never get planning permission.

Change the following sentences into indirect speech.

a. "I'll build the bungalow all the same." (Mr Craig said . . .)
b. "The bungalow isn't a bungalow at all but a stable." (He claimed . . .)
c. "Who's going to live in the bungalow?" (His neighbours asked him . . .)
d. "The bungalow will serve as a stable for Ricky, my pony. (Old Harry said . . .)
e. "It looks to me very much like a residential bungalow." (The council inspector told Harry . . .)
f. "Is the living room with the fireplace supposed to be used by the pony?" (The inspector asked Harry . . .)
g. "The fireplace will be used for blacksmith work." (Harry answered . . .)
h. "What does the pony need the fancy electric fittings in the bedroom for?" (The inspector wondered . . .)
i. "The electric fittings are there in case the horse gets ill and needs keeping warm." (Harry Craig said . . .)
j. "I think you're just trying to get round the planning restrictions. I'm afraid your bungalow will have to be pulled down." (The inspector said . . .)

24I **Frageanhängsel** (→ GIV35, 12F)

> The bungalow is for Harry when he retires, isn't it?

Add question tags to the following sentences.

a. He'll never get planning permission, ... b. He said he was building it for Ricky, ... c. You don't build bungalows for ponies, ... d. That place has a kitchen, a bathroom, a bedroom, and a living room, ... e. You've seen it yourself, ... f. This is a free country, ... g. He can build a stable with a living room and a bedroom if he wants to, ... h. There are women who leave thousands of pounds to cats and dogs, ... i. Old Harry has always had a screw loose, ... j. He wouldn't have got permission to build a bungalow on that plot, ... k. The bungalow will be pulled down, ...

24J **Bedingungssätze** (→ GIV19, 13H)

Please complete.

a. If you (not like) a job, you'll never do it well. b. I (be) absolutely furious if this was allowed to happen to any of my children. c. What would you do if you (know) that your next-door neighbour had gone away on holiday and left his dog in the house without food or water? d. I (be) grateful if you could give further details about the job as soon as possible. e. It might be all right if we just (have) the music without the commercials. f. If I'd been the director of the firm, I (not dismiss) Mrs Green. g. If the car had caught fire, I (be) trapped. h. If I'd ever had a son, I (want) him to turn out like you. i. He'd still be alive today if he (fasten) his seat belt before driving off.

24K **Hochleistungswort on**

I have no money **on** me *ich habe kein Geld bei mir*
on behalf of the committee *im Namen des Komitees*
on a cold winter night *an einem kalten Winterabend*
on one occasion *bei einer Gelegenheit*
I talked to her **on** the phone *ich sprach telefonisch mit ihr*
I'm not against it **on** principle *ich bin nicht aus Prinzip dagegen*
on production of your driving licence *unter Vorlage Ihres Führerscheins*
he moved there **on** his retirement *er zog dort bei seiner Pensionierung / beim Eintritt in den Ruhestand hin*
on the one hand . . . **on** the other hand *einerseits . . . andererseits*
she was dismissed **on** the spot *sie wurde auf der Stelle entlassen*
she had to cope **on** her own *sie mußte alleine fertigwerden*
the table **on** the right *die "rechtsstehende" (= nebenstehende) Tabelle*
Georgia borders **on** the Atlantic *Georgia grenzt an den Atlantischen Ozean*
comment **on** something *zu etwas Stellung nehmen*
get **on** the bus *in den Bus einsteigen*
pull a fast one **on** somebody *jemanden reinlegen / aufs Kreuz legen*
win £10,000 **on** the football pools *10000 Pfund im Fußballtoto gewinnen*
be dependent **on** other people *von anderen Leuten abhängig sein*
on wanting to leave the bathroom *als er / sie das Badezimmer verlassen wollte*
from 1922 **on** *von 1922 an*

24L General grammar test

a. I look forward . . . . . you in London next month.
 1. see 2. seeing 3. to see 4. to seeing

b. Instead . . . . . the fares, they reduced their services.
 1. of raising 2. raising 3. that they raised 4. to raise

c. She got a disappointing answer when she asked her boss for permission . . . . . on a two-week holiday.
 1. for going 2. of going 3. to go 4. to going

d. The lessons . . . . . from these stories can help you in your own lives.
 1. for being learnt 2. for learning 3. to be learnt 4. to learn

e. Do you enjoy . . . . . ?
 1. in travelling 2. of travelling 3. to travel 4. travelling

f. Her boss was understandably annoyed . . . . . left alone.
 1. about being 2. at being 3. being 4. for being

g. What happens if you park your car at a meter without . . . . . a coin in?
 1. putting 2. that you put 3. to put 4. you put

h. Dog breeding has become a . . . . . business.
 1. high profitable 2. high profitably 3. highly profitable 4. highly profitably

i. This advertisement would have made me . . . . .
 1. extreme suspicious 2. extreme suspiciously 3. extremely suspicious
 4. extremely suspiciously

j. It must be . . . . . for the driver to have music being blasted into his ear.
 1. downright dangerous 2. downright dangerously
 3. downrightly dangerous 4. downrightly dangerously

k. Dictators live . . . . .
 1. extreme dangerous 2. extreme dangerously 3. extremely dangerous
 4. extremely dangerously

l. If the car . . . . . fire, I'll be trapped.
 1. catches 2. caught 3. will catch 4. would catch

m. What would happen to the dog if its owner . . . . . ?
 1. died 2. dies 3. will die 4. would die

n. When . . . . . lunch?
 1. did you have 2. had you 3. have you got 4. have you had

o. They . . . . . over ten years.
 1. are now married for 2. are now married since
 3. have been married for 4. have been married since

24 M **Listening comprehension** ꝏ

Listen to the conversation on tape and decide whether the following sentences are True (T) or Not True (NT).

a. The story about the man who built a bungalow and said it was for a pony is a true story.
b. Janet says that arguments like the ones the pony owner gave are often used.
c. There has been a government act dealing with planning in England since 1971.
d. The man in the story would have to see two different councils about his building plans before he got permission.
e. Green belts are areas of land bought by the Government so that nobody builds on them.

f. The National Trust is a political organization but with private interests as well.
g. More than 55,000 people belong to the National Trust.
h. The National Trust owns nothing but land on which there are no buildings.
i. Only members of the National Trust are allowed to use the land belonging to the organization.
j. Three other organizations with similar aims to those of the National Trust are mentioned.

k. The main aim of the National Trust and the other organizations mentioned is to prevent countryside from being destroyed by building.
l. The idea of developing the new towns didn't start until after 1950.
m. The Government set up new towns because they didn't want old towns to be ruined by lots of new buildings.
n. The farmers who sold their land to the Government were able to get a high price because the Government had no other choice.
o. There will be twenty-four new towns in England when they've all been built.

p. About two million people now live in new towns, and over one million of them are young people.
q. Some of the new towns are now quite old, so most of the young people have been born and have grown up in them.
r. Old people who live in the new towns don't like them.
s. The new towns consist of lots of high-rise flats and nothing else.
t. The new towns offer attractive free-time entertainment.

25H Partizip Perfekt und -ing-Konstruktion in relativsatzähnlicher Funktion

Levi Strauss hoped to sell the canvas to miners **bound** for the gold fields.
He hoped to sell the canvas to miners **rushing** to the gold fields.

Please complete.

a. In 1906 an earthquake ..... by fire destroyed San Francisco's central area. b. The "California clippers" often covered their building costs with the profits ..... from a single trip to San Francisco. c. I'm looking for a lady ..... a red trouser suit. d. Among those ..... by the California Gold Rush was a 20-year-old German ..... Levi Strauss. e. The trousers ..... by the prospectors in the diggings had to be very strong to last. f. The stable ..... by Harry Craig looks very much like a residential bungalow to me. g. The council official ..... Harry's bungalow didn't believe a word of what old Harry said. h. The film ..... at the Odeon cinema is said to be very good. i. The children ..... this school are mostly from immigrant families. j. Crime is one of the main problems ..... the United States today. k. The information ..... in the prospectus is not quite correct.

25I Passiver Infinitiv

There was so much money **to be made** by shipping men and cargo to the gold fields that a whole new fleet of "California clippers" was built.
mit dem Transport von Menschen und Fracht . . . war so viel Geld zu verdienen

Please translate, using the passive infinitive.

a. Das Geld ist für ein neues Eisengitter zu verwenden.
b. Obwohl große Fortschritte gemacht worden sind, bleibt (noch) viel zu tun.
c. Der Hund war nirgendwo (*nowhere*) zu sehen.
d. Das war zu erwarten.
e. Diese Frage soll auf der nächsten Sitzung diskutiert werden.
f. Es ist keine Zeit zu verlieren.
g. Es war nichts zu machen.

25J **Adjektiv oder Adverb? Mit oder ohne -ly?** (→ GIV8)

Complete the sentences by putting in words from the following list.

bad/badly, cruel/cruelly, enormous/enormously, irrational/irrationally, popular/popularly, profitable/profitably, surprising/surprisingly, suspicious/suspiciously, unconscious/unconsciously

a. Denims have become amazingly ..... Denims are most ..... called jeans.
b. Her first novel ..... became an immediate success. Her first novel became ..... successful. The success of her first novel is ..... I consider the success of this novel .....
c. The food was ..... cooked. She's a ..... cook. She cooks .....
d. They spent an ..... sum of money on their new house. The firm has grown ..... during the last three years.
e. He was thrown out of the car and knocked ..... He was rushed to hospital .....
f. The letter made him ..... He studied the letter .....
g. It is ..... not to wear a seat belt but people often prefer to act .....
h. The new parking meters turned out to be anything but ..... Dog breeding has become a highly ..... business.
i. People who treat an animal ..... are not always punished. An animal may be destroyed if it would be ..... to keep it alive.

25K **Perfekt** (→ GIV17)

(Handlung begann in der Vergangenheit und dauert noch an.)

Please translate.

a. Wie lange sind Sie schon verheiratet?
b. Wie lange kennen Sie ihn schon?
c. Die Bibel ist seit mindestens 450 Jahren ein Bestseller.
d. Dieses (Theater-)Stück läuft (schon) seit vergangenem Oktober.
e. Ich fahre (schon) seit Jahren ohne Unfall.
f. Wir wohnen jetzt seit fünf Jahren hier.
g. Sagen Sie, wie lange sitzen wir hier (eigentlich) schon?
h. Ich fühle mich in letzter Zeit gar nicht gut.
i. Seine Freundin (*girlfriend*) zeigt ihm in letzter Zeit die kalte Schulter.

25L **Hochleistungswort of** (→ 12I)

what breed **of** dog is that? *was für eine Hunderasse ist das?*
hold the rank **of** lieutenant *im Rang eines Leutnants stehen*
attend a college **of** adult education *eine Volkshochschule besuchen*
write a letter **of** application *einen Bewerbungsbrief schreiben*
the majority **of** motorists *die Mehrheit der Kraftfahrer*
a large supply **of** canvas *ein großer Vorrat an Segeltuch*
fear **of** illness *Angst vor Krankheit*
arguments in favour **of** seat belts *Argumente (, die) für Sitzgurte (sprechen)*
be critical **of** something *einer Sache kritisch gegenüberstehen*
he is fond **of** animals *er hat Tiere gern / er mag Tiere (gern)*
be guilty **of** a crime *eines Verbrechens schuldig sein*
they are proud **of** him *sie sind stolz auf ihn*
be suspicious **of** something *einer Sache gegenüber mißtrauisch sein*
I informed him **of** the result *ich unterrichtete ihn über das Ergebnis*
persuade somebody **of** something *jem. von etwas überzeugen*
the committee is made up **of** 11 people *das Komitee besteht aus 11 Personen*

25M **Dictation exercise**

San Francisco, ... by the Spaniards after St Francis of Assisi, has a .... atmosphere .... different from that of .... other American city. Its ...., relaxed way of life and .... sights make it a .... with both American and .... visitors.
The best .... for .... San Francisco are spring and autumn (*Herbst*). Winter is .... warm, but in summer it can be .... cool when the late-afternoon .... comes in from the Pacific.
One of San Francisco's .... attractions are the cable cars, ... are not only an .... part of the .... transport system but also .... an easy and .... way of seeing the ....
In 1906, an earthquake .... by fire .... the .... of San Francisco's central ...., killing more .... 500 people. .... to recent .... by experts, another – .... even .... – earthquake could now .... at any time. The people of America's seventh largest city live ...., and they .... it.

26K To-Infinitiv, -ing-Form oder Präposition + -ing-Form?

The child was extremely small. (The child appeared . . .) The child appeared to be extremely small.
She used strong language on one occasion. (She admitted . . .) She admitted using strong language on one occasion.
He stole a camera. (He pleaded guilty . . .) He pleaded guilty to stealing a camera.

Change the following sentences as in the above examples.

a. So you stole all the articles here on the desk. (So you admit . . .)
b. She told her husband about it. (She couldn't avoid . . .)
c. The chairman asked her to describe the circumstances of her dismissal. (The chairman began . . .)
d. He didn't tell anyone about it. (He didn't dare . . .)
e. He persuaded the inspector that the bungalow was a stable. (He had no difficulty . . .)
f. She reads detective stories in her spare time. (She enjoys . . .)
g. They protested against the fare increase. (They went on . . .)
h. She had written to the company saying she had shoplifted certain articles in their High Street store. (It had been her intention . . . / She had intended . . .)
i. I'm seeing you in London next Friday. (I'm looking forward . . .)
j. She convinced them that the stealing had not been intentional. (She managed . . .)
k. They bought a bungalow at the seaside and moved there on retirement. (They made the mistake . . .)
l. He built a bungalow on the plot. (He got permission . . .)
m. He paid the fine. (He refused . . .)
n. I read that book many years ago. (I remember . . .)
o. She believes that dividends may go down as a result of shoplifting. (She's right . . .)
p. Stealing gives some people a thrill. (Stealing seems . . .)
q. I heard that dog skins are made into gloves. (I was shocked . . .)
r. They found a suitable flat in the city centre. (It was difficult . . ./They had difficulty . . . / They hoped . . . / They managed . . . / They tried . . . / They were unable . . .)

26 L Ask questions with how, how many, what, when, where, who, why.

Mrs Fielding lives at *27 Surrey Street.* Where does Mrs Fielding live?
Mr F. W. Davidson-Rose is Mrs Fielding's solicitor. Who is Mrs Fielding's solicitor?
Mrs Fielding pleaded guilty to *shoplifting wool and underclothes.* What did Mrs Fielding plead guilty to?

a. She stole these things *in Woolworth's.* b. She wanted to show *how easy it was to shoplift in Woolworth's.* c. Mrs Fielding wanted to draw the company's attention to *shoplifting losses.* d. *By becoming a shoplifter herself,* Mrs Fielding wanted to draw the company's attention to shoplifting losses. e. *The store detective* stopped her. f. She was stopped by *the store detective.* g. The store detective stopped her *as she was about to leave the store.* h. *Mrs Fielding* has shares in Woolworth's. i. She has *200* shares in Woolworth's. j. The policewoman treated Mrs Fielding *very politely.* k. People steal *because they are greedy, because they like to get things "on the cheap", because stealing gives them a thrill.*

26 M Genitiv (→ GIV1–2)

Please translate.

a. Ich habe dies bei Woolworth gekauft. b. Ist es leicht, in einem Kaufhaus wie Woolworth Ladendiebstähle zu begehen? c. Wir gehen Neujahr immer in die Kirche. d. Wir haben eine Woche an der See Ferien gemacht. e. In ein paar Tagen werden wir mehr wissen. f. Zum Bahnhof ist es zu Fuß etwa zehn Minuten. g. Ich habe heute beim Arzt einen Freund von Jim getroffen. h. Weißt du die Adresse von Walkers? i. Sind dies typische Frauenberufe? j. Das Fernsehen ist für die Augen kleiner Kinder schlecht.

"I – don't – know – what – came – over – me."

26N Saying the same thing differently

Ersetzen Sie die schräggedruckten Satzteile durch Formulierungen, die etwa dasselbe bedeuten.

a. Mrs Fielding *pleaded guilty to shoplifting* stationery, wool, toothpaste and *underclothes.* b. She wanted to *show* how easy it was to shoplift in Woolworth's. c. *It was my intention* to write to the company saying I knew for certain *shoplifting had been going on* at their Norwich *store* so they would *be forced* to do something about it. d. She *is a shareholder* in Woolworth's. e. I'm *convinced* my shares have been going down because of shoplifting. f. I'*m obliged* to warn you that *anything* you say will be taken down and may be used in evidence. g. Only *a very small fraction* of those caught are prosecuted and convicted. h. *Does shoplifting give people a thrill?*

26O Hochleistungswort by

sit **by** the side of the swimming pool *am Rande des Schwimmbades sitzen*
enter the house **by** the back entrance *das Haus durch den Hintereingang betreten*
the meeting should be over **by** 9.30 *die Sitzung dürfte bis 9.30 Uhr vorüber sein*
by that time he'll be gone *bis dahin wird er gegangen sein*
send a letter **by** airmail *einen Brief per Luftpost schicken*
by rail *per Schiene / mit der Eisenbahn*
inform somebody **by** telephone *jem. telefonisch benachrichtigen*
are you free **by** any chance? *sind Sie zufällig frei?*
answer **by** return (of post) *postwendend / umgehend antworten*
is that all right **by** you? *ist Ihnen das recht?*
the methods **by** which our children are taught *die Methoden, nach denen unsere Kinder unterrichtet werden*
he escaped the music **by** going downstairs *er entging der Musik, indem er nach unten ging*

Beachten Sie:
did you **pay** the bill / the milkman? *hast du die Rechnung / den Milchmann bezahlt?*
did you **pay for** the milk / the drinks? *hast du die Milch / die Getränke bezahlt?*

". . . followed by an afternoon's shoplifting in Oxford Street."

26 P **Dictation exercise**

22p store .... fined £50

A woman .... stole a 22p tube of toothpaste was fined £50 by Norwich magistrates.
Patricia Thompson, 54, of South Street, pleaded .... to .... the toothpaste from F. W. Woolworth in the High Street.
Police Inspector Roger Wade, ..., said that a security officer at the store .... Thompson take the toothpaste from a .... and .... it .... her pocket. She .... left and the security officer .... her ....
Thompson told the magistrates, "I have never .... anything like this .... I have not been .... well for some time. I am ...."

27G Vocabulary

admiration, calculate, deliver, fame, finger, instrument, inventor, lamp, palace, piano, refusal, rob, satisfy, unwilling

Complete the following sentences, putting in the correct forms of words from the above list.

a. Agatha Christie's novels brought her great . . . . . and a lot of money. b. As a result of the bank's . . . . . to give us a loan we are now in a very difficult situation. c. I bought the kids chewing gum, ice cream and chocolate, but they were still not . . . . . d. Two men . . . . . a bank in the High Street this morning, getting away with over £40,000 in one-pound and five-pound notes. e. Levi Strauss was the . . . . . of the kind of work pants now most popularly called "jeans". f. We are full of . . . . . for his courage. g. Please . . . . . the goods to our High Street branch. h. When they . . . . . how much the new building had really cost them, they were deeply shocked. i. He is . . . . . to accept a job at less money than he gets on the dole. j. The pianist couldn't play in the concert because he had broken a . . . . . k. He plays the trumpet and the . . . . . and several other . . . . . l. He parked his car right under a street . . . . . m. It's normal for a king or queen to live in a . . . . .

Goal scorer dies of joy

CAIRO, Saturday. – A soccer player died here as the result of scoring the winning goal for his team.

Reports say Aly Mahmoud Elefesh, 21, right winger for Elmasanea, died from nervous shock that resulted from overjoy and excitement. One report says he kept shouting "Goal . . . goal" until he fell unconscious.

He was transferred to a nearby hospital but died a few minutes later.

27H Turn the following statements into their opposites. Examples:

They *lost* the first match. They *won* the first match.

a. It was an *exciting* match. b. Brazil *beat* England. c. Our soccer season is *longer* and *more* strenuous than yours. d. The book was a *success.* e. The policeman arresting him was very *polite.* f. He's a born *loser.* g. It's a *densely* populated country. h. It's a rather *thick* book. i. She's very *neat.* j. *Everybody* wears jeans here.

27I Wortbildung: Adjektiv + -en = Verb

fast – **fasten** [fɑːsn]	soft – **soften** [sɔfn]	loose – **loosen**
hard – **harden**	tight – **tighten**	wide – **widen**
sharp – **sharpen**	weak – **weaken**	
short – **shorten**		long – **lengthen** ['leŋθn]
		strong **strengthen** ['streŋθn]

Put in the correct forms of verbs from the above list.

a. If the trousers are too long / short, you can have them . . . . . / . . . . .
b. If the belt is too tight, you can . . . . . it a little.
c. If the road is too narrow, it'll have to be . . . . .
d. The belt was far too loose, so I . . . . . it.
e. The long illness had . . . . . her, so the doctor recommended a medicine that would . . . . . her.
f. He used a knife ([naif] *Messer*) to . . . . . the pencil.
g. He might still be alive today if he'd . . . . . his seat belt before driving off.
h. The many defeats that he has suffered have . . . . . him.
i. He used to be very hard, but he's . . . . . since he got married.

27J Saying the same thing differently

a. The 1966 World Cup final was Ramsey's greatest *triumph.*
b. England's third goal became one of the most *hotly debated* in football history.
c. In Mexico they *were defeated by* Brazil and West Germany.
d. In 1973 they *failed to defeat* Poland.
e. The press *blamed* the team manager.
f. *The team manager is not to blame.*
g. We *suffered two defeats* before we *scored our first victory.*
h. People *were full of admiration for the team's successes.*
i. We expect *you to deliver* at the earliest possible date.
j. Alexander Graham Bell *was the inventor of* the telephone.
k. The two men just arrested are said to *have robbed a bank.*
l. Most of the people we asked *were unwilling* to help.
m. A secretary *ought to* be *tidy.*

West Germans interested in football
In February 1977, 27% of the West German population were "very interested", 31% were "a little interested", and 42% were "not interested" in football.

27K **Hochleistungswort for**

will you join us **for** dinner? *wollen Sie zum Essen zu uns kommen?*
he did that **for** fear of being sacked *er tat das aus Angst entlassen zu werden*
jail someone **for** life *jem. auf Lebenszeit inhaftieren*
people steal **for** all sorts of strange reasons *Leute stehlen aus allen möglichen seltsamen Gründen*
do you know that **for** certain? *wissen Sie das ganz bestimmt / sicher?*
for once the meters weren't all taken *ausnahmsweise waren die Parkuhren nicht alle besetzt*
men bound **for** the gold fields *Männer auf dem Wege nach den Goldfeldern*
we headed **for** Frisco Bay *wir hielten Kurs auf die Bucht von San Francisco*

27L **General grammar test**

a. Ramsey, ... very popular with the press, was blamed for the England team's failures.
1. who had never been 2. who has never been 3. whom had never been 4. whom has never been

b. The powerful bosses of the Football Association, with some of . . . . . Ramsey had never been very popular, dropped him like a hot potato.
1. which 2. who 3. whom 4. whose

c. Ramsey, ... the Queen had knighted in 1967, was sacked in 1974 because of the England team's failures.
1. which 2. who 3. whom 4. –

d. When Helmut Schön retired in 1978, he . . . . . coach of the West German national soccer team for 14 years.
1. had been 2. has been 3. was 4. was being

e. By the time he retired in 1978, Helmut Schön . . . . . one of the world's most successful football coaches.
1. became 2. becomes 3. had become 4. has become

f. If Poland had not lost to West Germany, they . . . . . the 1974 World Cup.
1. may have won 2. may win 3. might have won 4. might win

g. How long . . . . . this pain, Mr Walker?
1. are you having 2. do you already have 3. have you 4. have you had

h. You'd better . . . . . in bed for a day or two.
1. if you stayed 2. stay 3. staying 4. to stay

27M **Listening comprehension** ꝏ

Read the newspaper article in 27H again, then listen to the conversation on tape and decide whether the following sentences are True (T) or Not True (NT).

a. The newspaper article in 27H that is being talked about here is invented and is not from a real English newspaper.
b. One of the speakers suggests the footballer might have died of a heart attack.
c. One of the speakers used to be a professional footballer.
d. The former footballer used to play hard and practise and be coached a lot.
e. He doesn't think any of the people he played with could have had a heart attack while playing.

f. Both speakers agree that football clubs are chiefly interested in pounds and pence.
g. Both speakers agree that football players are only interested in money.
h. One of the speakers doesn't think professional sport should really be described as "sport" nowadays.
i. Both speakers agree that football players are rich.
j. One of the speakers says some football clubs run cinemas as well.

k. One of the speakers says people don't go to football matches just to watch football.
l. He says fans like being part of a crowd because it makes them feel strong.
m. He says fans don't like having to declare their identity in a crowd.
n. The football match one of the speakers talks about ended in a draw.
o. He says he was pushed and hit by fans.

p. According to the text, it was George Orwell who said that crowds are ugly.
q. One of the speakers agrees that all crowds are unpleasant.
r. George Orwell thought sport helped countries to make friends with each other, according to the text.
s. Both speakers agree with what George Orwell said about international sport.
t. Fans at an international football match see the match only as a competition between the two teams of footballers, according to George Orwell and the speakers.

28K To-Infinitiv, Infinitiv ohne to, -ing-Form oder Präposition + -ing-Form?

She	asked	him	**to stop**	smoking.
She	made	him	**stop**	smoking.
She	saw	him	**smoke / smoking**	a cigarette.
She	stopped	him	**from smoking**	in the non-smoker.

Make sentences as in the above examples, using the correct forms of the words given.

a. they / let / she / sleep / in the living room
b. they / allow / she / sleep / in the living room
c. they / invite / she / sleep / in the living room
d. they / do not / mind / she / sleep / in the living room
e. they / do not / want / she / sleep / in the living room
f. he / hear / she / cry / for help
g. he / prevent / she / cry / for help
h. he / stop / she / cry / for help
i. she / do not mind / he / drink / one or two pints of beer in the evening
j. she / do not want / he / drink / so much
k. she / get / he / give up / drinking
l. I / can't imagine / he / say / such a thing
m. she / leave / he / sit / on the ground
n. we / see / a man / beat up / a young woman in the street
o. he / signal / I / remain behind
p. she / remember / he / put / the key in his coat pocket
q. the robbers / force / he / give / them all the money he had in the house
r. she / help / he / fill in / the questionnaire

28L Passiv der Sätze in 28K (→ GIV25)

He	was asked	**to stop**	smoking.
He	was made	**to(!) stop**	smoking.
He	was seen	**to(!) smoke**	a cigarette.
He	was seen	**smoking**	a cigarette.
He	was stopped	**from smoking**	in a non-smoker.

Change the following sentences in 28K into the passive: b, c, f, g, h, m, n, q.

(Einf. Form) He **travels** daily on the underground.
(Verlaufsform) He **was travelling** on the underground when he had the heart attack.

(Einf. Form) Dozens of cars **are towed** away by the police every day.
(Verlaufsform) Look, your car **is being towed** away by the police!

Signale für einfache Form: Feststellung einer Tatsache – keine Betonung des Ablaufes – Gewohnheit – Regel – "immer so".
Signale für Verlaufsform: Betonung des (augenblicklichen) Verlaufs – "jetzt gerade" – "vorübergehend, nicht immer so" – "noch andauernd" – "vorläufig" – Ausnahme, nicht Regel.

Please complete.

a. With the number of smoking cars reduced, smokers (often break) the regulations unashamedly while most non-smokers (suffer) in silence.
b. It's terribly hot here at the moment. My wife especially (suffer) very much from the unusual heat.
c. This idea came to me while I (work) at the kitchen sink.
d. Nowadays, people (work) much less at the kitchen sink than they used to.
e. I (certify) that the above statements are true and complete.
f. Her English (improve) fast and she'll soon be able to take up a job as a secretary in the export department.
g. The students attending the intensive courses (usually find) that their English (improve) fast.
h. I'm glad to say that Frank's English (begin) to improve.
i. We (have) a lovely time. The hotel is very pleasant and the weather is fine.
j. We (have) a flat in the city centre now.
k. We (pass) a lonely cottage halfway up the hill when we suddenly heard a woman's voice crying for help.
l. This book (show) American life as it really is.
m. Do you remember that lovely day in London – it was warm, the sky was blue, we (sit) in an open car and you (show) us the sights.
n. At present I (learn) English at evening classes in preparation for a forthcoming trip to Australia.
o. A lot of people (learn) English at evening classes.

28N **So + Hilfsverb ("auch")** (→ GV1)

I work ninety hours a week, and **so does** my wife. *und meine Frau auch*
I am very busy at the moment, and **so is** my wife. *und meine Frau auch*
I've got a good knowledge of French, and **so has** my wife. *und meine Frau auch*

Complete the following sentences as in the example.

The press blamed Ramsey personally for England's failures, and so did the powerful bosses of the Football Association.

a. Their English is improving, and . . . . . their job prospects. b. Jack is fed up, and . . . . . I. c. The camera is stolen property, and . . . . . the pocket calculator. d. He was very aggressive, and . . . . . his dog. e. I was shocked, and . . . . . all the other people who were there. f. I travel daily on the underground, and . . . . . my wife and children. g. Poirot bowed, and . . . . . the other men in the room. h. We've got a dog, and . . . . . the people next door. i. He has an egg-shaped head, and . . . . . his son. j. Petrol will become more expensive, and . . . . . everything else. k. He could read at the age of four, and . . . . . his brother. l. You should always be strapped to your seat, and . . . . . your children.

28O **So / neither + Hilfsverb ("auch" / "auch nicht")** (→ GV1)

"I'm very busy." – **"So am I."** *ich auch*
"I'm not aggressive." – **"Neither am I."** *ich auch nicht*

Add answers with So . . . or Neither . . . as in the examples. ꝏ

a. "I travel daily on the underground." b. "I didn't get a word of apology." c. "I don't like to break the regulations." d. "I can't understand him." e. "I'm going by ship." f. "I haven't read anything by Agatha Christie." g. "I always have lunch in the canteen." h. "I'd thought it was a bungalow, not a stable." i. "I'd have accepted if they'd asked me." j. "I wouldn't have been against it on principle." k. "I watched a lot of TV as a child." l. "I should really give up smoking." m. "I wouldn't like to live here."

28P **Hochleistungswort from**

A is different **from** B *A ist anders als B*
A differs **from** B *A weicht von B ab / A unterscheidet sich von B*
judging **from** this letter *diesem Brief nach zu urteilen*
learn a lesson **from** something *eine Lehre aus etwas ziehen*
we must prevent him **from** doing that *wir müssen ihn daran hindern, das zu tun*
prohibit people **from** smoking *den Leuten das Rauchen verbieten*
stop someone **from** smoking *jem. davon abhalten zu rauchen*

28Q **Dictation exercise**

RULES FOR GIVING UP SMOKING

1. Always .... a cigarette when it is .... to you – this weakens the influence other .... have in .... you to smoke.
2. .... one packet of cigarettes at a time, never more.
3. Every time you .... cigarettes, ... a different brand – this will weaken the hold a .... brand has on you.
4. Wait .... after breakfast – or longer – before smoking your first cigarette. This will weaken the .... smoking routine you have fallen into.
5. Slowly .... to ten before you light a cigarette. This helps to .... the automatic actions you have .... over the years.
6. After each cigarette put the packet ....
7. If you run out of cigarettes, never let .... give you one.
8. Slowly .... the number of places and situations where you don't smoke: ...., in bed, before meals, while driving, while watching TV, etc.
9. Always .... your cigarettes in another room so you have to make an .... to get them.
10. Never smoke a cigarette more .... halfway down.
11. If you .... a cigarette, wait five – ten – fifteen minutes before having one.
12. Never smoke .... after meals; wait .... you have left the table.
13. Don't smoke .... you are waiting for someone or something.
14. When you smoke, stop doing all other things, i.e. do not watch TV, ..., work, drink, etc.
15. Always sit on an .... chair .... smoking.

29I **Need** (→ 6M, 6N)

The answers given by you **need not** all be true. *brauchen nicht alle zu stimmen*
They **don't need to** work for a living. *brauchen nicht für ihren Lebensunterhalt zu arbeiten*

Wie diese Beispiele zeigen, kann *need* sowohl "unvollständig" (wie z. B. *can, must*) als auch "vollständig" (wie z. B. *want, hope*) konstruiert werden.
Weitere Beispiele:

We *needn't* go (, *need* we?) We *don't need to* go (, *do* we?)	*Need we* go? (No, we *needn't.*) *Do we need to* go? (No, we *don't.*)

Change the following sentences as in the above examples.

a. You needn't tell us what you saw.
b. I needn't be told how to do it.
c. You needn't show me any other ones.
d. You really needn't send a telegram.
e. He needn't help us, need he?
f. We needn't discuss this problem now, need we?
g. Need he really come back?
h. Need I tell you anything else? – No, you needn't.
i. Need he put on a tie? – No, he needn't.

29J **Need to ≈ have to**

We needn't go (, need we?) (We don't need to go [, do we?]) We don't have to go (, do we?)	Need we go? (No, we needn't.) (Do we need to go? [No, we don't.]) Do we have to go? (No, we don't.)

In sentences like the ones above *need to* and *have to* have about the same meaning. Do the sentences in 29I once again, using *have to* instead of *need to.*

29K **Please complete.**

a. Ireland (achieve) independence from Britain in 1921. b. Ireland (divide) since 1921. c. The I.R.A. (want) Northern Ireland to be reunited with the Irish Republic. d. Since 1968 Protestants and Catholics (be) engaged in a violent struggle, which (claim) over 1200 lives by 1975. e. Ross McWhirter, the co-editor of the *Guinness Book of Records* (murder) in November 1975. f. Only nine days before Ross McWhirter's murder, two people (kill) when terrorists (throw) a bomb through the window of a crowded London restaurant. g. On January 2, 1978, it (announce) that violent deaths in Ulster (drop) by nearly two-thirds in 1977 (compare) with 1976; the total (be) the lowest since 1970: 111 people (kill) in terrorist actions against 297 the previous year. h. On February 17, 1978, a terrorist time-bomb explosion at an East Belfast restaurant (kill) 12 guests and (injure) 30 while they (attend) a special sporting function.

29L **Verlaufsform des Passivs**

Is Northern Ireland **being forced** to remain a part of the U.K.?
wird Nordirland gezwungen . . .?
The debris from the bomb explosion **is being cleared up** by detectives of the Bomb Squad. *wird weggeräumt*
The same size of loaf **is being sold** at our local supermarket. *wird verkauft*

Change the following sentences into the passive.

They are increasing the tax on cigarettes.
The tax on cigarettes is being increased.

a. They are reducing the number of smoking cars on underground trains.
b. Are you shortening or lengthening these trousers?
c. Soccer fans are still debating the question of whether it was a goal or not.
d. American cities are increasingly electing black mayors.
e. They're making her book into a film.
f. The firm that's publishing my new book is in Vienna.
g. The music they're playing on the buses seems to be acceptable to the majority.
h. The bungalow that Harry Craig is building up Thrush Lane is supposed to be a pony stable.

"We are claiming responsibility for the nice quiet day you've had today in Belfast."

29M **-ing-Form mit eigenem Sinnsubjekt** (→ GIII35, 17G)

They **voted in favour of Ulster continuing** the union with Great Britain.
sie stimmten dafür, daß Ulster die Union mit Großbritannien fortsetze
55% of all West Germans **would be in favour of capital punishment being** introduced for terrorists.
wären dafür, daß für Terroristen die Todesstrafe eingeführt wird

Please translate.

a. Die Mehrheit ist dafür, daß Ulster ein Teil Großbritanniens bleibt.
b. Ich erinnere mich daran, daß er etwas darüber sagte.
c. Wir müssen verhindern, daß es wieder passiert.
d. Entschuldigen Sie, daß ich frage – aber wo haben Sie Ihr Englisch gelernt?
e. Was für eine Situation führte dazu, daß er das Tier so grausam behandelte?
f. Was war ihre Reaktion darauf, daß er zum Leutnant befördert wurde?

29N **Hochleistungswort up**

clear **up** the debris *die Trümmer / den Schutt wegräumen*
he climbed **up** the tree *er kletterte auf den Baum*
drink **up** your beer *trinken Sie Ihr Bier aus*
drive **up** to a petrol station *an einer Tankstelle vorfahren*
he got **up** from his chair *er stand von seinem Stuhl auf*
the price of petrol is going **up** *der Preis für Benzin steigt / geht in die Höhe*
make **up** stories *sich Geschichten ausdenken*
sit **up** straight! *setzt euch gerade hin!*
I'm flying **up** to Glasgow tomorrow *ich fliege morgen rauf nach Glasgow*
he's **up** in Glasgow at the moment *zur Zeit ist er oben in Glasgow*
high **up** in the mountains *hoch oben in den Bergen / im Gebirge*
he isn't **up** yet *er ist noch nicht auf*

New words in the dictation exercise on page 147:
screen = the part of a television on which the picture appears (*Bildschirm*)
rubbish = something that is absolutely no good, useless, without value, stupid (*utter rubbish = totaler Mist*)
bullet = a small piece of metal that is shot from a gun (*Kugel*)

Television has .... the world into one great .... People everywhere .... what is happening everywhere else, they can watch it happen on .... television screens in their living rooms.

.... the western world people watch the same American-made ...., crime ...., thrillers and Westerns. "Bonanza" and "Lassie" are .... to hundreds of millions of people in about a hundred countries.

In the .... of many experts, British and West German television are among the best in the world. The TV .... of these countries are .... for the quality of .... documentaries, plays, ... magazines, and educational programmes.

But even the best .... produce many .... of utter rubbish every day, and for someone who watches one of the more stupid programmes it is easy to understand why the TV is also .... the "idiot box".

Many people are .... about the effects of TV .... on children. One expert tells the story of a .... boy who asked his father for .... bullets for his gun because he wanted to kill his little sister "the way they do on television".

"Would you like to wait? Mr Brindsley is still being kidnapped by the first group of terrorists."

30L **Stellung der Objekte** (→ 13G)

	Indirektes Objekt	Direktes Objekt	**Indirektes Objekt**
a. He sent / bought	**Judy**	red roses.	
b. He sent / bought		red roses	**to / for the girl he had met at the Green Banana.**
c. He sent / bought	**her**	red roses.	
d. He sent / bought		red roses	**to / for her.**
e. He sent / bought		them	**to / for her.**
f. He sent / bought		them	**to / for Judy.**
(*Aber nicht:* *He sent / bought Judy them.)			

Beachten Sie die Stellungsmöglichkeiten für das indirekte Objekt:
Ohne *to / for* vor dem direkten Objekt (a, c).
Mit *to / for* nach dem direkten Objekt (b, d, e, f).
In der Regel steht das längere und/oder betontere Objekt hinten.
Ist das direkte Objekt, nicht aber das indirekte Objekt ein Pronomen, so ist nur die Stellung f möglich.

Verben, die zwei Objekte haben können
Vom Typ send (nachgestelltes indirektes Objekt mit *to*):
bring, give, leave, offer, owe, pay, read, recommend, sell, show, teach, tell, write.
Vom Typ buy (nachgestelltes indirektes Objekt mit *for*):
build, choose, cook, fetch, find, get, make, play, reserve, win.

Please translate.

a. Kannst du mir das Buch bringen? b. Kannst du mir das Buch bringen, das auf dem Tisch im Wohnzimmer liegt? c. Kannst du es mir geben? d. Kannst du es Jack geben? e. Kannst du dies Buch dem Verkäufer geben, der uns gestern bedient hat? f. Ich schulde Jack £100. g. Diesen Betrag schulden wir Jack, nicht der Bank. h. Sie hinterließ ihr ganzes Geld dem Milchmann. i. Sie hinterließ ihm ein Vermögen. j. Sie hinterließ es ihrem Sohn. k. Er kaufte ihr ein Wörterbuch.

l. Er kaufte Wörterbücher für alle, die eins brauchten. m. Er kaufte jedem seiner Kinder eins. n. Er kaufte es ihr. o. Koch mir eine deiner herrlichen chinesischen Suppen! p. Er verkaufte den Anhänger einem Kollegen, der eine große Familie hat. q. Warum willst du ihn nicht Jack verkaufen?

30 M **Indirektes Objekt stets mit to**

Bei *describe, explain, report, suggest* und einigen anderen Verben wird ein etwaiges indirektes Objekt stets mit *to* angeschlossen.

	Direktes Objekt	**Indirektes Objekt**
The courier explained	the hotel's facilities	**to the guests.**
You should have reported	the mugging	**to the police.**
She couldn't describe	the dress	**to the others.**
I've suggested	some improvements	**to the manager.**

Change the above sentences as in the following example.

He explained	the method	to the parents.
He explained	it	to the parents.
He explained	the method	to them.
He explained	it	to them.
The method	was explained	to the parents.

30 N **Please translate.**

a. Er zeigte ihr das Haus.
b. Er beschrieb ihr das Haus.
c. Er zeigte ihr das Haus, das ihm angeboten worden war.
d. Er beschrieb ihr das Haus, das ihm angeboten worden war.
e. Können Sie uns ein Hotel in Killarney empfehlen?
f. Können Sie uns eine bessere Lösung vorschlagen?

"Willie, we've been married for over thirty-five years now. Don't you think it's time we gave some thought to divorce?"

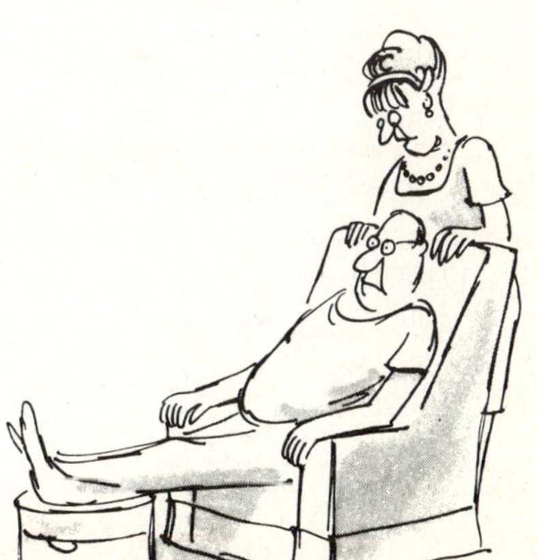

30O "Sehr" (→ GV13)

Put in: very, very much, much.

a. She's losing her looks . . . . . fast.
b. I like her . . . . .
c. His poems have been . . . . . praised by the critics.
d. They have . . . . . different ideas of what to do in their spare time.
e. Her husband has to work . . . . . hard.
f. I would be . . . . . in favour of the second solution.
g. He's . . . . . frustrated in his present job. He finds the work . . . . . frustrating. The work seems to frustrate him . . . . .
h. Your father seems to have been . . . . . annoyed.
i. I hope you aren't suffering too . . . . . from the heat.
j. Her presence seems to stimulate him . . . . . He seems to find her presence . . . . . stimulating.

30P Hochleistungswort get. – Put in the correct forms of get.

a. In Ulster, the terrorists . . . . . shopkeepers to pay them protection money so their shops aren't bombed. b. . . . . . round the planning restrictions won't be easy. c. He had difficulty . . . . . back into the stream of traffic. d. I must have lost the glove while . . . . . off the bus. e. I was held up at the very last moment and couldn't . . . . . to the airport in time. f. He sleeps till noon and has downed his first glass of brandy by the time he . . . . . out of bed. g. . . . . . around Malta is easy and cheap: by bus, by taxi, or by horse-drawn cab. h. We still have no idea how the burglars . . . . . into the house. i. My husband, who didn't know I had it on my shopping list, ... an identical one from a small shop off Parliament Street. j. They probably wouldn't have . . . . . a divorce if there had been any children. k. It's really surprising. The older she . . . . ., the more active she becomes. l. My husband didn't tell me too soon because he knows how excited I . . . . .

30Q Hochleistungswort about

disagree **about** something *über etwas verschiedener Meinung sein*
why don't you do something **about** it? *warum ändern Sie nichts daran?*
dream **about** something / someone *von etwas / jemand träumen*
quarrel **about** something *sich über etwas streiten*
wander **about** the park *im Park umherwandern*
he was **about** to leave *er war im Begriff abzureisen / wollte gerade abreisen*

30 R General grammar test

Choose the correct forms. Note: In this test, sentences may have more than one correct answer.

a. He celebrated his pools win with ..... friends at the Green Banana.
   1. a dozen of 2. dozen of 3. dozens 4. dozens of
b. There ..... people at yesterday's meeting.
   1. have been about two dozen 2. have been about two dozens of
   3. were about two dozen 4. were about two dozens of
c. The return fare is ..... single fare.
   1. double of the 2. double the 3. the double 4. the double of the
d. The driver has to keep ..... on things behind him in the bus.
   1. an eye 2. his eye 3. his eyes 4. the eyes
e. I ..... High Street yesterday.
   1. have met him in 2. have met him in the 3. met him in 4. met him in the
f. I'm sorry ..... temper this morning.
   1. I lost my 2. I lost the 3. I've lost my 4. I've lost the
g. The I.R.A. wants ..... reunited with the Irish Republic.
   1. Northern Ireland being 2. Northern Ireland for being
   3. Northern Ireland to be 4. that Northern Ireland is
h. He admitted ..... some cameras from the photographic department.
   1. stealing 2. to have stolen 3. to having stolen 4. to stealing
i. Cigarettes are a product that should by normal standards be .....
   1. impossible to be sold 2. impossible to sell 3. impossibly to be sold
   4. impossibly to sell
j. Many blacks live in homes that ..... a table for the children to do their homework on.
   1. don't even have 2. even don't have 3. even have not 4. have not even
k. You're a pensioner. You ..... work for a living any more.
   1. don't have to 2. don't need to 3. mustn't 4. needn't
l. The Government wouldn't dare to do that, ...?
   1. do they 2. does it 3. would it 4. would they
m. May I suggest ..... downstairs?
   1. that you will go 2. you go 3. you going 4. you to go
n. Some non-smokers have suggested ..... altogether.
   1. abolishing smoking cars 2. smoking cars to be abolished
   3. that smoking cars should be abolished 4. to abolish smoking cars

o. . . . . . who wanted Ulster to continue the union with Britain.

1. It was the Protestants 2. It were the Protestants

3. The Protestants was it 4. The Protestants were it

p. "I wonder what the next little treat for the unemployed will be," . . . . .

1. one angry newspaper reader wrote. 2. one newspaper reader wrote angrily. 3. wrote one angry newspaper reader. 4. wrote one newspaper reader angrily.

q. "Don't ask me why I smoke," . . . . .

1. grimly said the jeans-clad sportsman. 2. said the jeans-clad sportsman grimly. 3. the jeans-clad sportsman grimly said. 4. the jeans-clad sportsman said grimly.

"I don't know why we come here – the service is terrible."

Schlüssel zu den Übungen

1N **a.** They formed a chain to pour water over the whale. **b.** They stopped in Orpington to visit the Garnetts. **c.** He went out to get some exercise. **d.** She went to London to take an English course. **e.** He wrote (to them) to thank them for their present. **f.** She went to the station to meet Brian. **g.** She bought the newspapers to have something to read on the plane. 1

1O I'm looking forward to meeting Jane and Frank again. I'm looking forward to seeing some good new plays at the theatre. I'm looking forward to hearing a concert at the Royal Festival Hall. I'm looking forward to taking pictures of the sights of London. I'm looking forward to doing some shopping in Oxford Street and Regent Street. I'm looking forward to drinking beer and playing darts in a riverside pub.

1P **a.** to buy. **b.** to come. **c.** to go. **d.** to pick. **e.** having. **f.** answering. **g.** to travel; to walk. **h.** watching. **i.** to think. **j.** earning / to earn. **k.** learning / to learn. **l.** learning. **m.** to pay. **n.** Watching.

1Q **a.** She said she had to be there at six o'clock. **b.** They said they always had a spare bed for Bill. **c.** She said she lived in a suburb of London. **d.** They said they were interested in the project. **e.** He said his plane arrived at 18.25. **f.** He said he'd be staying with friends. **g.** He said he'd send it under separate cover. **h.** He said that wouldn't be necessary.

1R **a.** Seats will have to be booked early. **b.** Accommodation will have to be arranged. **c.** This letter will have to be translated. **d.** Our reservation at Brown's Hotel will have to be cancelled. **e.** These letters will have to be sent today. **f.** The texts for the new catalogue will have to be got ready.

1T **a.** Could you please put me through to the ticket counter. **b.** It could be worse. **c.** How could she do this to me? **d.** He might think we're afraid of him. **e.** Shall we say ten o'clock? **f.** What shall we do tonight? **g.** The meeting should be over by 9.30 / by half past nine. **h.** Smoking shouldn't be allowed here. **i.** That shouldn't have happened.

1V *Dear* Brian and Shirley, *Just* a short note to let you *know* that I got back *safely*. The *flight* was very *pleasant* and, as *expected,* both Rita and our dog, Bello, were waiting for me at the airport. *Once* again many thanks for *letting* me stay with you. I *enjoyed* every minute of the time we *were* together. We hope you'll *keep* your word and visit us on your way *south* during the summer *holidays*. *Love* from Rita. And please give my *regards* to the boys. Yours ever, Günter.

1W **a.** through. **b.** in / during. **c.** by. **d.** with; in; of. **e.** to; at. **f.** with; in. **g.** about; of. **h.** on. **i.** by. **j.** by / with; on. **k.** At / In; to.

2H **a.** My daughter is getting married in January. **b.** We're going to a concert at the Royal Festival Hall tonight. **c.** Gerry is coming to see us this afternoon. **d.** When are you going to Malta? **e.** We're 2 spending the summer holidays in Swanage this year. **f.** When are we arriving at Heathrow? **g.** The bar is closing in a few minutes. **h.** The Prime Minister is visiting France at the end of this month. **i.** When are you moving into your new house? **j.** It's Friday, so we're having fish for dinner today. **k.** What are you doing tomorrow? **l.** We're watching television this evening.

2I **a.** you'll / you will. **b.** we'll / we will. **c.** I'd / I would. **d.** you'll / you will. **e.** I'd / I would. **f.** wouldn't / would not. **g.** you'll / you will. **h.** wouldn't / would not.

2J **a.** arrives. **b.** gave. **c.** won. **d.** does not / doesn't. **e.** were not / weren't. **f.** go. **g.** had. **h.** were not / weren't.

2K **a.** I'm visiting / I'll be visiting / I'm going to visit / I'll visit / I will visit / I shall visit Glasgow next January. I visited Glasgow last October. **b.** The Taylors have been living / have lived in Glasgow for about ten years now. They moved to Glasgow about ten years ago. **c.** We have just received / We've just received your letter of April 10. We received your letter yesterday. We get dozens of such letters every day. **d.** C. and A. have been married for over ten years now. They got married ten years ago. Their marriage has been very happy so far. When are R. and B. getting married? / When will R. and B. be getting married? / When are R. and B. going to get married? / When will R. and B. get married? **e.** I've never seen this shop before. How long has it been here? It was opened last Wednesday. It's a discount bookshop which sells books at half their normal price. **f.** Where did you buy it? I bought it at Foyle's. I always buy my books at Dillon's in Malet Street. **g.** Hatchard's, London's oldest bookshop, has been at 187 Piccadilly since 1767. **h.** Will you be free / Are you free on the morning of the 20th? I have / I'm having / I'm going to have a meeting at my office at 8.30. When do you think the meeting will be over? Well, the last time that man came to see me he stayed till lunch. **i.** I played a lot of football when I was young. Nowadays I never play football. I've been playing / I've played tennis ever since I gave up football. He's playing tennis. He's been playing tennis since about two o'clock.

2L **a.** About three weeks ago we placed an order for £265 worth of goods. The goods we ordered three weeks ago have not arrived yet / have not yet arrived. Please let us know when you sent off / will send off the goods we ordered three weeks ago. The goods you ordered on March 7 will be sent off within the next three days. **b.** My holiday starts the day after tomorrow. Oh, how nice. Where are you going? / Where will you be going? To America. A tour of the East Coast, starting in Boston. We're flying / We'll be flying from Heathrow. The flight will take / takes about seven hours. I must be going now. My wife is waiting / will be waiting for me.

2M **a.** How old do you think he is? **b.** When do you think this book was published? **c.** Where do you think you get better service . . .? **d.** Why do you think that happens? **e.** How do you think he usually passed the day? **f.** Where do you think he stayed when he was in Glasgow? **g.** Why do you think he visited them? **h.** Why do you think they don't want to get married?

2N **a.** Could we also come at eight? **b.** We would be so glad if you could come. **c.** Carl Sandburg's father could not write his own name. **d.** On wanting / When he wanted to leave the bathroom, he found that he could not open the door. **e.** Will you both be able to come? **f.** He will have to do without me while I am away. **g.** Does one have to book the seats in advance? **h.** I don't know why I should get married. **i.** I was (supposed) to spend the night at a hotel near the airport.

2P **a.** about. **b.** on. **c.** for. **d.** on. **e.** for. **f.** on. **g.** on; for. **h.** since; to. **i.** at; of. **j.** on; at. **k.** On; at; to. **l.** by; on; on.

2Q Dear Carol and Alan, *Thank* you very much for the *lovely* dinner yesterday. We both enjoyed it a lot. It was *delightful* to meet so many old *friends* again, and we *particularly* enjoyed looking at the film taken of your wedding ten years ago. It's a *pity* Ann and Stephen *couldn't* come. It *would* have been nice to see them again after all these years. If you *should* ever come to our part of the *country,* you must look us up. If you can bring the *children,* so much the better. Tell them *they'll* find lots of *entertainment* here: a dog and two cats, *chickens,* some cows, and even a pony to *ride* on. There are also *woods* to play in and a lake not too far away where they *could* go *swimming* or boating. All good *wishes,* Yours ever, John and Sandra.

3I **a.** What are the languages spoken in Malta? **b.** What makes Malta particularly attractive to students of English? **c.** What did their courier tell them about? **d.** What sea is Malta surrounded by? **e.** What is Malta's winter like? **f.** What was the weather like? **g.** How did she get here? **h.** How do they spend most of the day? **i.** When does the next group of tourists arrive? **j.** When did Malta become independent from Britain? **k.** Where did they stay? **l.** Why won't they be able to come? **3**

3J **a.** any; something. **b.** any. **c.** some. **d.** some. **e.** any. **f.** any; some. **g.** some. **h.** any. **i.** anybody. **j.** somebody. **k.** anybody. **l.** something.

3K **a.** warmer. **b.** nicer. **c.** more interesting. **d.** more optimistic. **e.** better. **f.** better or worse. **g.** more often. **h.** more difficult. **i.** more. **j.** less. **k.** more boring and tiring.

3L **a.** swiftest; slowest. **b.** hottest; wettest; driest. **c.** happiest. **d.** most popular. **e.** most intelligent. **f.** best. **g.** worst / biggest. **h.** most. **i.** least.

3M **a.** Getting around is easy and cheap: by bus, by taxi, or by horse-drawn cab. **b.** Smoking is bad for the / your health. **c.** Watching television / TV can harm the development of young children. **d.** Working on the assembly line is very tiring. **e.** Dancing is something I hate. **f.** There's dancing every night at this hotel. **g.** Eating in / at a restaurant is more expensive than eating at home. **h.** Finding a hotel room in London is difficult at this time of the year.

3N **a.** correct. **b.** I sent / took the damaged recorder back to them. **c.** They've ordered 250 . . . **d.** She likes Stephen very much. **e.** Malta is (particularly) popular with British holidaymakers. **f.** Malta's institutions and everyday life are very much like England's / are very similar to England's. **g.** The courier gave them information about their rooms, about sporting and recreation facilities, entertainment, etc. **h.** There's dancing from 9.45 p.m. to 2.45 a.m. every night / every night from 9.45 p.m. to 2.45 a.m. **i.** How did you spend the day? **j.** We're having a wonderful / lovely time. **k.** They've just got back / come back from Malta.

3P Malta became *independent* from the United Kingdom in 1964. There are about as many *people* living in the Maltese *islands* as in Luxemburg, which has an *area* over eight times as *large*. The *largest* of the *islands,* Malta, is about the *size* of the city of *Cologne*. Malta has a *Mediterranean* climate with hot summers and warm winters. The Maltese *people* are of *mixed* race. The *languages* spoken by them are Maltese and English. The *large* majority of the population belong to the *Roman* Catholic *Church*. There are three English and three Maltese *daily* newspapers and three *Sunday* newspapers. Malta's main *trade* partners are *Britain,* Italy, and West Germany. Tourism is *becoming* more *important* every year.

3Q Rent for TV in hotel room: 50p per day. Hotel shop's opening hours: 9 in the morning till 8.30 at night / 9 a.m.–8.30 p.m. Foreign newspapers available after: 5 in the afternoon / 5 p.m. Foreign magazines available after: Friday morning. Breakfast served from 7.30 to 9.30. Breakfast in bed: order from waiter in restaurant. Sporting facilities: (heated) swimming (pool), (2) tennis (courts), table tennis, sauna. Janet Stratford available: mornings 11–12.30; evenings 6.30–8.

3R **a.** with. **b.** from. **c.** around; by. **d.** for. **e.** from. **f.** to / for; in. **g.** from; since. **h.** by; of; with; in; on; beside. **i.** to; about.

4

4I **a.** The doctor wants him to stay in bed for the next few days. **b.** We're appealing to neighbours everywhere to keep an eye on old people living alone. **c.** Do you expect us to enjoy ourselves? **d.** Can't we get her to fetch Billy from school every day? **e.** I asked them to send us their latest catalogue. **f.** I told him to phone the emergency medical service. **g.** What led the police to believe that Mr Cole had been dead for five months? **h.** What made her write to a newspaper about her experience?

4J English is not an easy language to learn. For those interested in souvenirs, gold and silver objects are the things to bring home from Malta / to look out for. If there's no hotel, we must find some other place to sleep. Immigrants have difficulty finding a decent place to live. My husband is not an easy man to live with / to talk to. On the promenade at the seaside you always have something to do / to look at / to see. She's an interesting person to talk to. Some old people don't have enough money to live on. That was a silly thing to do. There are many historical sights to look at / to see. This company has an interesting job to offer. This is a good song to sing. What are suitable souvenirs to bring home from Malta / to look out for?

4K **a.** You / They should have phoned the emergency medical service. **b.** That shouldn't have happened. **c.** That's something you shouldn't have missed (out). **d.** The milkman can't have put the bottles in the fridge. **e.** You could have stayed / lived with us. **f.** We could have taken the eight o'clock train from St Pancras. **g.** She couldn't have opened the window alone. **h.** He may have waited at / in the office. **i.** A holiday in Malta might have been quite different. **j.** The situation might have become dangerous. **k.** You must have seen the old man.

4L *Dozens* of people *saw* him, but nobody *stopped* to help the old man who was sitting on the ground *leaning* against a wall in the High Street at about 7 *p.m. Deathly* white and trembling, he was *obviously* unable to help himself. Had he *suffered* a *heart* attack? There were some *youths* across the road *outside* a shop that was still open. They must have *seen* the old man, but they *didn't* take any notice. At last, the old man was *seen* by a woman *carrying* a *basket* and a small dog. She *tried* to help him to his *feet,* but he was much too *weak.* So she left him *sitting* on the ground and went and *phoned* the *emergency* medical service.

4M **a.** a short time / while ago. **b.** where he lived. **c.** wasn't strong enough. **d.** It was obvious that he was very ill. **e.** rang. **f.** Dozens of people saw him. **g.** young men / people on the other side of the road. **h.** Somebody / Someone told me / I heard. **i.** We're asking neighbours. **j.** She is very poor / lives in poverty. **k.** She never meets other. **l.** comes to see. **m.** It is possible that he died.

4N **a.** week. **b.** ice. **c.** dark. **d.** weak. **e.** child. **f.** friends. **g.** chair. **h.** painful. **i.** believes. **j.** high. **k.** long; wide; deep.

5I **a.** He's probably picked up. **b.** She sings beautifully. **c.** Please get me a doctor quickly. **d.** Malta is rapidly becoming. **e.** prepared everything carefully. **f.** The policeman obviously reported / Obviously the policeman reported. **g.** I know them very well. **h.** he certainly didn't show it. **i.** You really don't know. **j.** He did the whole job carelessly. **k.** I often / sometimes / never go by taxi. **l.** What do you like especially / What especially do you like about Malta? **m.** Who still believes. **n.** He was sitting comfortably / comfortably sitting. **o.** she cried happily. She told him happily. **p.** The dog always barks loudly when. **5**

5J mind telling; tried to lift; remember seeing; seemed to be; busy talking; offer to help; to be; helped her (to) carry; took us about half an hour to get him there; promised to get; any chance of phoning.

5K **a.** When they were found, the letters had been lying there . . . **b.** Neighbours said (that) Mr Cole had always been very independent. **c.** When I met her in the hotel lobby, she'd / she had only just arrived. **d.** By 1974 Malta had been independent for ten years. **e.** By the time he was forty, they'd / they had been living together for five years.

5L **a.** I want you to (have / take a) look at this book here. **b.** Would you like us to spend our honeymoon in Malta? **c.** He wants us to look after the old gentleman. **d.** Would you like me to tell you something about the hotel's facilities? **e.** I'd like you to meet a nice girl with similar interests. **f.** I want you to take your feet off the table. **g.** I want you to stop work, now that we're getting married. **h.** I'd like us to wait till / until the court case is over.

5M **a.** Will you be able to come to Susan's wedding? **b.** I'm afraid I won't be able / I'll be unable to come. **c.** If / When we go to Malta, we'll be able to talk / speak a lot of English. **d.** If we spend all our money on drinks, we won't be able / we'll be unable to buy any souvenirs. **e.** When she lives / is living here, her grandchildren will be able to visit her almost every day. **f.** Will she be able to manage her household alone? **g.** Her relatives won't be able / will be unable to look after her. **h.** We hope we'll be / to be able to prevent tragedies like this in future.

5N **a.** don't forget. **b.** What's his job? / What does he do? **c.** difficult. **d.** Who did she marry? **e.** telephone operator. **f.** He asked her for a date. **g.** I didn't know. **h.** He's an attractive man. **i.** Do you have. **j.** He wrote that he couldn't come.

5P *Fancy* the way my *friend* Susan Williams met her *husband,* Michael! He was the *policeman* who *reported* her when she had that *nasty* car accident last year. He was very *kind* to her because she was so *dazed* and *shaken,* but he also questioned her *thoroughly,* and when he *found* that the accident was her *fault,* he booked her for *careless* driving. *Later* he gave *evidence* against her in *court.* For Michael it had *been* love at first *sight,* but he didn't show it. It wasn't *until* the *court* case was over that he *phoned* her and *asked* her out. After *their* first *few* dates they *knew* they were going to *stay* together, and last *month* they got married – *almost* a year to the day since the accident that *brought them* together.

6

6J **a.** standing / sitting. **b.** showing. **c.** looking. **d.** lying. **e.** living. **f.** working. **g.** answering. **h.** going. **i.** questioning / asking. **j.** attending / taking.

6K **a.** mentioned / described. **b.** given / contained. **c.** spoken / used. **d.** advertised. **e.** predicted. **f.** offered. **g.** invited. **h.** made / sold. **i.** requested / required. **j.** paid.

6L **a.** After finishing primary school at the age of eleven, I attended . . . **b.** After studying at Oxford, he became . . . **c.** After eating a light supper, I went . . . **d.** After pottering about in the garden for about two hours, he joined . . . **e.** After phoning the emergency medical service, she went . . . **f.** After getting married at St Giles Church, West Bridgford, they went . . . **g.** After serving in the U.S. Navy for six years, Carter returned . . . **h.** After questioning her thoroughly, the policeman reported . . . **i.** After finishing her meal, Elaine discovered . . .

6M **a.** The crash need not / needn't be . . . **b.** You need not / needn't phone . . . **c.** This form here need not / needn't be . . . **d.** We need not / needn't have . . . **e.** You need not / needn't bring . . . **f.** We need not / needn't tell . . .

6N **a.** No, we / you needn't. **b.** No, we / you needn't. **c.** No, you needn't. **d.** No, it needn't. **e.** No, they needn't. **f.** No, it needn't. **g.** No, they needn't.

6O **a.** Is it necessary for us to go to the meeting? – No, it isn't. **b.** Is it necessary for us to arrange accommodation for him? – No, it isn't. **c.** Is it necessary for me to be absolutely punctual? – No, it isn't. **d.** Is it necessary for it to be an intensive course? – No, it isn't. **e.** Is it necessary for the underwear and pyjamas to be ironed? – No, it isn't. **f.** Is it necessary for the room to be air-conditioned? – No, it isn't. **g.** Is it necessary for these questions to be answered too? – No, it isn't.

6P **a.** He is a U.S. citizen. **b.** The author of this book, Peter Underwood, is President of the Ghost Club. **c.** From 1962 to 1966 Carter was a member of the Georgia Senate. **d.** From 1971 to 1974 he was Governor of Georgia. **e.** As a bus driver one earns / you earn about £80 a week. **f.** I've got / I have a headache. **g.** The boy has (got) a temperature. **h.** I've got / I have a pain in my back. / I've got / I have pains in my back. **i.** It's a pity (that) we can't go to Malta for our holiday / spend our holiday in Malta. **j.** What a surprise! **k.** What kind of beer do they / people drink here / is drunk here?

6Q **a.** That's quite a difference. **b.** That's quite a long / rather a long way. **c.** What a wonderful tree that is! **d.** It took us / We took about half an hour. **e.** Why is Malta such an attractive place / so attractive a place? **f.** Many a liberal has become a conservative.

6R Georgia (so named after the English king George II) was *founded* in 1733, and in *1788* became the *fourth* state of the United States. About 8 *per cent* of Georgia's population work in *agriculture.* Peanuts, cotton, maize, and *tobacco* are the *main* agricultural products. The *climate* of Georgia is mild, with temperatures between an *average* winter minimum of 5 *degrees* and an *average* summer maximum of 33 *degrees.* Georgia's *capital,* Atlanta, a *fast-growing* modern city with a population of about half a million, *elected* its first black *mayor* in 1973. Atlanta has *various* institutions of *higher* education, *among* them the Georgia Institute of Technology, which was founded in *1888.* One of the *world's* most popular products, Coca-Cola, comes from Atlanta. The *famous* drink was first mixed there by Dr S. Pemberton in *1886.* Today the Coca-Cola Company sells over *175* million *bottles* a day in more *than* 130 *countries.*

6S **a.** 1. **b.** 4. **c.** 4. **d.** 4. **e.** 2.

7H **a.** The body was discovered by a neighbour. **b.** He was mugged by a gang of youths in a New York subway station. **c.** The Sydney Opera House was designed by Joern Utzon. **d.** The phone was answered by her mother. **e.** She was interviewed by a reporter from the *Evening Herald.* **f.** The girl's screams were heard by Mrs Harris. **g.** This letter was written by Mark Twain. **h.** The little girl was bitten by an Alsatian. **7**

7I **a.** They shouldn't be allowed to watch television. **b.** It must be kept spotlessly clean. **c.** It can't be turned on till June the tenth. **d.** The windows ought to be kept closed. **e.** It can't be sold at this price. **f.** Can these letters be translated? **g.** Can't the room be given to someone else? **h.** Won't the air conditioning be turned on? **i.** Shouldn't he be met at the airport? **j.** What time must the tickets be picked up?

7J **a.** Carter was elected in 1976. **b.** The Sydney Opera House was opened in 1973. **c.** The cost is / The costs are estimated at 7 million dollars / $7,000,000. **d.** The abbreviation *Ms* is increasingly used nowadays / is (being) used increasingly nowadays. **e.** The room has been given to someone / somebody else. **f.** The dog had been cruelly treated / treated cruelly by its owner / master. **g.** The windows have to be / must be kept closed / shut. **h.** I don't think (that) he'll be re-elected.

7K **a.** The President has been in office for almost a year now. **b.** My father has been in hospital for exactly ten days now. **c.** The house has been unoccupied since Mrs Nelson died. **d.** We've had our swimming pool for two years now. **e.** I've had this account since I moved here three years ago. **f.** I've wanted to visit Glasgow since you wrote to me in January. **g.** How long have you lived at this address? **h.** For how many years have you been employed at Interoil?

7L **a.** The Hendersons have been living in Harlington for two years now. **b.** These old books have been lying here for at least three months now. **c.** We've been learning English for over two years now. **d.** The boy has been running a temperature since he came back from the excursion. **e.** I've been looking out for a suitable souvenir since I arrived. **f.** She's been suffering from sleeplessness since she had that accident last May. **g.** Susan and Michael have been dancing together since they came. **h.** My wife has been playing tennis since the club was founded about three years ago. **i.** How long have you been attending this school? **j.** How long has Dr Brown been treating you? **k.** How long have you been feeling like this?

7M **a.** We've been married (for) a quarter of a century (now). **b.** How long have you had this pain / these pains? **c.** How long has your father been in hospital? **d.** How long have you been watching TV / television, children? **e.** I haven't been feeling at all well lately. **f.** He has been living here / He has lived here (for) three years (now). **g.** I've been playing football since I was ten. **h.** I've been learning English for three years (now).

7N Australia is over *thirty* / *30* times the *size* of West Germany but has less *than* a *quarter* of West Germany's population. *Eighty* / *80* per cent of Australia's population live in cities; *thirty-eight* / *38* per cent in and *around* Sydney and Melbourne alone. Australia's national income per person is *almost* the same as West Germany's; it is much higher *than* Austria's but lower *than* Switzerland's. Australia's *seasons* fall at *different* times of the *year* from Central Europe's: spring is from September to December, summer from December to *March,* autumn from *March* to June, and winter from June to September.

7O Mrs Wilson arrives *home* on the evening when she *found* the old man lying in the street. She tells her husband what has *happened.* **Mr W** Who have you just *phoned*? – **Mrs W** The emergency medical service. – **Mr W** The emergency medical service! *Why*? – **Mrs W** Well, you see, on my way home I *found* an old man lying in the road – well, not actually lying in the road, he was *sitting* on the ground, against a wall, *leaning* against a wall, you see. In the High Street it was, outside Woolworth's. – **Mr W** Oh dear. Accident? – **Mrs W** No, he was ill, very ill. He was all *deathly* white and *trembling* all over. – **Mr W** What did you *do* then? – **Mrs W** Well, he was very *weak,* and I'm not very strong of course, so I couldn't *help* him up, up on to his feet. And *then* I had my shopping basket and the dog with me, too. – **Mr W** Well, you could have put them down, *couldn't* you? – **Mrs W** Hm, yes, I suppose I *could.* I didn't think. I was so excited. Well, anyway, I couldn't *help* him up so I *asked* him what his name was and where he *lived.* Well, he managed to *tell* me that, so I *left* him there where he was, *sitting* on the ground, and went and *fetched* his wife. I was lucky; they *only* lived a few hundred yards away. – **Mr W** Yes, that was lucky. And what *then*? – **Mrs W** Well, I *fetched* his wife and *between* us we managed to get him *along* to his home. It *took* us nearly half an hour. – **Mr W** Phew! Half an hour for 300 yards? – **Mrs W** Yes, he was so heavy, you *see.* Well, anyway, we *got* him home and then I came home and, well, you know the *rest,* I've *just* rung the emergency medical service. I *hope* he's going to be all right. – **Mr W** Yes. – Didn't anybody help you carry the old man *home*? – **Mrs W** Well yes – no they didn't. I mean, that's the point. Dozens of *people* saw us – pedestrians and *motorists.* There was a shop that was still *open,* you *see,* and quite a lot of people stopped there, and there was a *group* of youths outside, too. – **Mr W** But nobody *helped* you. – **Mrs W** Nobody. – **Mr W** And we are a Christian *country.* I mean, we always say we are, *don't* we? Why don't you *write* to the paper about this? – **Mrs W** Hm, I think I *will.*

7P **a.** (3). **b.** (1). **c.** (2). **d.** (1). **e.** (2). **f.** (2). **g.** (3).

8 8G **a.** a; the. **b.** – / a. **c.** the; –. **d.** –; the. **e.** a; a. **f.** the; a. **g.** a; a / –. **h.** –; –; –. **i.** –; –; the. **j.** –. **k.** –; the; –. **l.** a; a. **m.** –. **n.** the; –; –; a; – / a. **o.** a; the; –.

8H **a.** Experts pointed out that the pictures were unsuitable for ten-year-olds. **b.** The teachers responsible argued that the textbooks showed people as they really were. **c.** Parents said that they didn't want their children to read texts reflecting moral and political attitudes quite different from their own. **d.** Teachers defended the use of such reading materials by saying that they might help children in their own lives. **e.** An angry mother complained that the texts used in her son's school contained a lot of violence, sex scenes, and gutter language. **f.** A teacher reacted by saying that the Bible also contained a lot of violence, sex, and strong language.

8I **a.** He asked her why she hadn't written earlier. **b.** He wondered who had won. **c.** They wanted to know how long it had taken to build the bridge. **d.** They had no idea when Susan was getting married. **e.** He asked her what her name was. **f.** She wondered why the windows had to be kept closed. **g.** He asked me if / whether I would be in London for the wedding. **h.** She asked him if / whether he would be able to meet her at the airport. **i.** The engineers were asked if / whether the foundations would be strong enough to hold the roof. **j.** She wanted to know if / whether the play was any good. **k.** The teacher asked her if / whether she liked that sort of poetry. **l.** She asked him if / whether he had filled in the questionnaire.

8J **a.** He said his name was Harris. **b.** The manager thought I was drunk. **c.** He asked her if / whether he could take her out / go out with her. **d.** She told me that the play was no good and that the gardener was the murderer. **e.** The author asked his publisher how his latest novel was selling. **f.** She wrote (that) she was a mother of four herself. **g.** He told me (that) his father had been absolutely furious. **h.** The teacher told us that our children were (being) taught by a very progressive method.

8L **a.** Carter comes *from* Georgia. He was born *in* / *at* Plains *on* October 1, 1924. Georgia lies north *of* Florida and borders *on* the Atlantic. Carter got married *at* the age *of* twenty-two. He studied *at* the Georgia Institute *of* Technology and the U.S. Naval Academy. Carter became President because he was very popular *with* the masses. **b.** When one asks parents what they think *of* their children's school textbooks, one finds that many people are critical *of* the texts contained *in* them. Our children are taught *by* the most progressive methods, but according *to* Mrs Watson, who works *in* the personnel department *of* a large company, an increasing number *of* youngsters applying *for* work are neither literate *nor* numerate. As a result *of* this sort of experience, many people are becoming suspicious *of* "progressive" methods.

8M Sir, Like many *other* parents of teenage children I am becoming *increasingly* worried by the textbooks used in *our* schools. I find it *disturbing* that there should be so many texts *containing* violence, sex *scenes* or "gutter" language. Often *enough* the reading material *reflects* moral and political *attitudes* quite different from *those* of the *majority* of parents. The *teachers* defend these books by saying that they *know* better *than* parents what kind of texts are *suitable* for children, that the *new* textbooks are progressive and have been *praised* by experts, that they *show* life as it *really* is, and that the *lessons* to be learnt from them can help the children in *their* own *lives.* I *know* that times have *changed* since my own school days and that the textbooks used *then* may not be *suitable* for *today's* youngsters, but *isn't* it *wrong* if some of the texts used *nowadays* seem to *destroy* the values the children are *taught* at home? Yours *faithfully,* Susan Cole.

9I **a.** to bring. **b.** to buy. **c.** to serve / serving. **d.** meeting. **e.** to hear. **f.** telling; to get. **g.** to meet. **9**
h. to be; working / to work. **i.** to seeing. **j.** of being. **k.** wondering; to spend. **l.** to hear. **m.** to pay. **n.** to know. **o.** of being. **p.** working. **q.** to meet. **r.** of phoning. **s.** to drink / drinking. **t.** to think. **u.** of spending; of going. **v.** to find.

9J **a.** Shopping in the crowded streets and markets is great fun. **b.** Finding a decent place to live is difficult. **c.** Having people like The Samaritans is important. **d.** Coming to your home was a particular pleasure for me. **e.** Is committing suicide a crime? **f.** Pottering about in the garden all day doesn't satisfy you in the long run. **g.** Getting him along to his home took them about half an hour. **h.** Watching too much television can be harmful for the eyes. **i.** Being unable to manage one's own household must be hard. **j.** Getting a divorce will cost you a lot of money.

9K **a.** possibly. **b.** wisely; expensive; generous / expensive. **c.** wise / possible / good; terribly. **d.** hard; helpless; hardly. **e.** easily. **f.** well. **g.** well. **h.** well / easy.

9L **a.** Can / May I help you? **b.** He can repair / is able to repair the machine himself. **c.** We are now able to live / can now live off the interest. **d.** How could she do this / that to me? **e.** He wanted to go out, but he couldn't open / was unable to open the door. **f.** They couldn't find / were unable to find the kind of work they had been trained for / the kind of work for which they had been trained. **g.** He was able to repair the machine himself. **h.** Will you be able to translate this letter? **i.** I'm afraid we won't be able to come. **j.** He may still be at home. **k.** Do you know where he is? – No, but he might / could still be at the office. **l.** His address may have changed. **m.** He can't have repaired the machine himself.

9M When Jim Mitchell *won* £170,000 on the *pools* two years ago, he didn't *lose* his *head.* Most of his *winnings* have been *invested,* and Jim, his wife Betty, and *their* three children live *off* the *interest.* The *win* hasn't *changed* the family *very much.* Jim still drinks his 2½ *pints* at the pub *round* the corner *twice* a *week,* and the Mitchells haven't *been* on any spending *sprees* or *bought* the *traditional* bungalow. Of *course,* there are now things the Mitchells can do *which* they couldn't do *before* they *won* the *pools.* For *example,* right after Jim *received* the *cheque* from *actress* Laura McDonald, he *took* his wife on a three-and-a-*half*-month *cruise round* the world, and this *year* they are *planning* to spend four *weeks* touring *Australia.*

9O **a.** T. **b.** NT. **c.** NT. **d.** T. **e.** NT. **f.** T. **g.** NT. **h.** NT. **i.** T. **j.** NT.

9P **a.** I'm not fond of pottering about in the garden and walking around / about Manchester all the time. **b.** In. **c.** As; through. **d.** on; on; round; off. **e.** On the day I got the cheque for £185,000, I treated all my mates at / in the factory to champagne.

10 10J **a.** isn't she? **b.** is it? **c.** isn't it? **d.** was it? **e.** weren't you? **f.** couldn't it? **g.** haven't you? **h.** do you? **i.** didn't you? **j.** does it? **k.** did he? **l.** don't you? **m.** did you?

10K **a.** have. **b.** don't. **c.** shouldn't. **d.** hadn't. **e.** am. **f.** do. **g.** does. **h.** will. **i.** hadn't. **j.** can. **k.** couldn't. **l.** do. **m.** couldn't / shouldn't. **n.** did. **o.** wasn't. **p.** hadn't. **q.** did. **r.** should / are / will. **s.** was. **t.** did / could / should. **u.** would.

10L **a.** Give it up! **b.** Wherever did you pick up that fascinating little book you sent us for Christmas? **c.** (*Betonung auf* taking out:) Michael is taking Susan out. / (*Betonung auf* Susan:) Michael is taking out Susan. **d.** Are you sure I have to fill them all in? **e.** Why don't you read out to us the letter Susan has written from Malta? **f.** . . . before he writes it out. **g.** How long does it take to get back a car that has been towed away? **h.** You can ring up the owner of the car at this number. **i.** We can't say anything before we've tried out the new method suggested by them.

10M **a.** What is meant by "gutter language"? **b.** Who are these scarves made by? **c.** Youngsters / Young people under eighteen are not permitted / allowed to drive a car. **d.** My car was towed away. **e.** This book has been praised by (the) critics. **f.** This kind / sort of book might / could be regarded as completely unsuitable for youngsters / young people.

10N **a.** got. **b.** do you have. **c.** in the way. **d.** little. **e.** returned / came back; disappeared. **f.** rang (up). **g.** writes out. **h.** Hold on / Hang on. **i.** Since. **j.** left. **k.** Perhaps; little. **l.** if you show.

10P I *thought* I *wouldn't* be long. After all, I *just* wanted to *buy* a *birthday* present for my wife – a scarf or something – at Selfridges in Oxford Street. As *usual* all the parking meters *were* taken, but *there* was an *empty* space on the corner of Duke Street and Wigmore Street. That's *where* I parked my car. It *wasn't* very much in the way *there,* and I *thought* I would be back *within* a *few* minutes, so it *wouldn't* matter. As it happened, a traffic warden *saw* me parking my car, made a *note* of the time, and later *reported* it to the police as *"causing* an obstruction". The police *were* very quick – much quicker *than* I was *choosing* a scarf for my wife – and when I *finally* came back to *where* I had parked the car, it was *gone.* At first I *thought* it had been *stolen,* but *then* someone told me he *saw* it *being* towed away. So I *phoned* the police and was told my car had been *taken* to the car pound in Park Lane and I could *collect* it *there* "on production of my driving *licence* and certificate of *insurance*". When I *gave* the scarf to my wife on her *birthday,* I *didn't* tell her how much it had *cost* me. I *just* said: "This is not an *ordinary* scarf. *Getting* it *wasn't* as *easy* as you *might* think."

11K He had all the plans changed. I want to have an information sheet drawn up. I'll have everything arranged. The police had the door opened. They had the book sent under separate cover. Why do you want to have your dog destroyed? I'll have the leather made into gloves. Etc. **11**

11L **a.** They had the toaster repaired. **b.** He had a seat booked on the morning plane. **c.** The police had the car towed away. **d.** He had copies sent to all the members of the committee. **e.** I'll have the bill cancelled. **f.** We must have / We'll have to have some photos taken. **g.** I'll have to have the letter translated.

11M **a.** –. **b.** who. **c.** that / which. **d.** who. **e.** who; that / which. **f.** whose. **g.** that / which. **h.** –. **i.** which. **j.** who. **k.** whose; that / which. **l.** that / which. **m.** –. **n.** –. **o.** who. **p.** which. **q.** who.

11N **a.** city centre / town centre. **b.** at the shops in the city centre / town centre. **c.** proved to be. **d.** discovered something. **e.** Wait a moment. **f.** You ought to know that when you travel in Quebec. **g.** It was easy / not difficult for him to explain it. **h.** She does her job very well / works very efficiently.

11O **a.** to think. **b.** seeing. **c.** for wanting. **d.** of going. **e.** to expire. **f.** for learning. **g.** marrying. **h.** wondering. **i.** to drive. **j.** to be.

11P **a.** The TV / television programmes are getting / becoming worse and worse. **b.** Pocket calculators are becoming cheaper and cheaper. **c.** The film was becoming more and more interesting. **d.** More and more old people have to live / are having to live in old people's homes. **e.** More and more people are moving to the suburbs. **f.** He works / is working more and more and earns / is earning less and less.

11Q When the town fathers of Whitehorse, Canada, had parking meters *installed* in the downtown *area,* these *were* simply *ignored* by motorists. The town fathers had no *choice* but to *hire* an energetic meter maid, who had to *patrol* the streets checking the meters and *issuing* tickets to parking *offenders.* The meter maid was so *efficient* that more and more customers *stayed* away from the downtown stores and did *their* shopping at a shopping *centre* outside the town. To *prevent* their customers from doing *their* shopping *elsewhere,* a large downtown department store *hired* an "anti-meter maid", *whose* job it was to make the *same* round as the meter maid and put *coins* in all the meters that *were* about to *expire.*

12

12E **a.** Yes, she's happier than she's ever been before. **b.** Yes, it's more practical than the smaller size. **c.** Yes, it's more beautiful than any other arts centre I know. **d.** Yes, it's longer than her husband's. **e.** Yes, it's more difficult than where you live. **f.** Yes, it was more sensible than what her husband did. **g.** Yes, it's better than my previous job. **h.** Yes, it's dearer than at any of the other shops. **i.** Yes, it's more alarming than most people think. **j.** Yes, he drinks more than anyone else in the family. **k.** Yes, I'm feeling worse than when I came an hour ago.

12F **a.** wasn't it? **b.** didn't you? **c.** isn't it? **d.** don't they? **e.** can't they? **f.** did he? **g.** doesn't it? **h.** are you? **i.** aren't you? **j.** don't they? / haven't they? **k.** is it? **l.** can you? **m.** are they? **n.** have you? **o.** was there?

12G **a.** some. **b.** something. **c.** any. **d.** anyone. **e.** any. **f.** anybody. **g.** any. **h.** anybody. **i.** some. **j.** something. **k.** someone. **l.** any. **m.** anything. **n.** any. **o.** somebody. **p.** something. **q.** some. **r.** anything. **s.** something. **t.** something / anything.

12H **a.** What do you do when / if you're in a hurry? / What does one do when / if one is in a hurry? **b.** It's terrible when / if one has / you have nothing to do. **c.** If you park your car in the middle of the road, it will be towed away / it gets towed away / it is towed away. **d.** What does one do if one is unable to manage one's own household? / What do you do if you are unable to manage your own household? **e.** A driving licence is a document that says / a document saying that you are / one is allowed to drive a car. **f.** The noise drives you out of your mind. **g.** How can such tragedies be prevented? / How can one prevent tragedies like this / that? **h.** Letters and (news)papers up to five months old were found behind the front door. **i.** Which hospital was he taken to?

12I **a.** I left primary school at the age of ten. **b.** They spent the rest of their lives in a bungalow at the seaside. **c.** He was the hero of the nation. **d.** Can you give me the number of the Queen's Hotel? **e.** I have a good knowledge of French. **f.** Quebec City is the capital of the province of Quebec. **g.** Malta is a member of the Council of Europe. **h.** The island of Gozo is (a) part of the republic of Malta. **i.** She bought two pounds of apples and a bottle of tomato ketchup.

12J *Bread* made by the same *bakery* is sold at different prices by different shops. A *loaf* that sells at 20p at a small shop may cost as *little* as 15p at a supermarket. The supermarket is *usually* cheaper *than* the corner shop because it *buys* things in large *quantities* at great *discounts.* But it also happens that an *article* costs less at a small shop *than* it *does* at a large store. So it *pays* to shop *around,* but many *people* are unable to do that because they are too *busy. Comparing* prices is *easy* as long as you have things that are *completely* identical. If, for *example,* a *particular* brand of *tomato* ketchup costs 34p per *bottle* at shop A and 28½p at shop B, then you *know* that B is cheaper *than* A. But what do you do when there are six different brands of washing powder on the *shelf* at the supermarket and they are all different prices? To *decide* which washing powder is the best *value* for money, you have to *know* what *differences* in quality, if any, there are and *whether* the *packets* are all the same *size.* Even if you had that information, it *would* still be *difficult* to say *exactly* which washing powder is the best *bargain.*

12K **a.** NT. **b.** T. **c.** T. **d.** NT. **e.** NT. **f.** T. **g.** T. **h.** T. **i.** T. **j.** T. **k.** NT. **l.** T. **m.** NT. **n.** NT. **o.** T. **p.** NT. **q.** T. **r.** T. **s.** NT. **t.** T.

13H **a.** What would we have done if the Alsatian had attacked the child? **b.** What would you have done if you had been in Mr Duffield's position / place? **c.** He would have been absolutely furious if that had happened. **d.** If the dog had not found a new owner, it would have been destroyed / killed. **e.** If you had bought him a drink, he would not have become / got so aggressive. **f.** If we had been younger, the money would have changed / altered our lives. **g.** If Dennis Bryan had been more sensible, he would not have left his wife. **h.** If Dennis had not met Judy, he would not have divorced his wife. **i.** If he had stayed with his wife, he would not have become an alcoholic. **13**

13I **a.** This may be just the right thing for you. **b.** May I visit him in hospital? **c.** You may park your car here for a limited time. **d.** You may find the following words and expressions useful. **e.** A new car of this type may cost you £3,000. **f.** I may be able to get back into my old job at Empire Machines. **g.** A court may order the destruction . . . **h.** People who are in despair may always ring The Samaritans. **i.** May tickets be booked in advance? **j.** A policeman may cause an injured animal to be destroyed. **k.** He may still be sleeping. **l.** It may have been towed away. **m.** Under the Protection of Animals Act of 1911 an animal may not be kept without food or water.

13J **a.** shall. **b.** should go / ought to go. **c.** Should. **d.** is to. **e.** should. **f.** Shall. **g.** was to. **h.** Shall. **i.** should. **j.** was to / should. **k.** Shall. **l.** am to. **m.** should. **n.** is to. **o.** shall.

13K **a.** What. **b.** What. **c.** Which / What. **d.** What. **e.** Which. **f.** Which. **g.** what / which. **h.** What. **i.** what. **j.** What. **k.** Which. **l.** What. **m.** Which.

13L **a.** was. **b.** left. **c.** banned. **d.** fined. **e.** has been. **f.** put. **g.** be. **h.** taken.

13N Two greyhounds that *arrived* at London's *Heathrow* Airport *were* both very ill after *being* flown from Ireland in *boxes* that were *too* small and *badly* ventilated, Uxbridge magistrates *heard* today. One of the dogs was in a box shorter *than* itself, and the other in a box *which* made it *impossible* for the dog to stand *properly,* it was *said.* A dogs' home *attendant* said both *boxes* had grilles *too* small for ventilation, and *there* was blood around one grille *where* the dog had *tried* to chew its way *through.* An *airline* official *said* the dogs had not *been* carried in a way *likely* to *cause* them *unnecessary* suffering and injury.

14L **a.** He's always ready to help them. **b.** The Olympic Games are due to open on 19 July. **c.** We were sorry to hear that your flight was not very pleasant. **d.** At the moment he's busy planning his next trip. **e.** If you should require any further information, please do not hesitate to let me know. **f.** Is this advertisement likely to attract suitable candidates? **g.** I enjoy meeting lots of people. **h.** He refuses to think about the future. **i.** I remember learning that poem at school. **j.** They were disturbed to find texts . . . **k.** The parking meters turned out to be anything but profitable. **l.** She went on telling them stories. **m.** The plans made by the architect proved to be very difficult. **n.** Then it was my turn to buy the drinks. **o.** Would you mind answering me a few questions? **p.** He had the cheek to tell me there was a lot of money to be saved by buying the jumbo size. **q.** The flying time seems to be very short. **r.** Malta has the advantage of being a English-speaking country. **s.** He arranged to meet Mr Stewart . . . **t.** I managed to find out his name and address. **u.** They decided to bring in a law against the killing of dogs for their skins. **v.** He always found reasons not to accept / for not accepting them. **w.** We'll look forward to seeing you on the 20th, then. **x.** He pleaded guilty to causing unnecessary suffering to . . .

14M **a.** I wrote this postcard (while) sunbathing by / at the side of the swimming pool. **b.** He wrote them a letter asking for further details. **c.** The boy spends a lot of time watching television / TV. **d.** Instead of phoning for an ambulance, they carried the old man home. **e.** He parked his car at a (parking) meter without putting a coin in. **f.** After eating some / a few sandwiches, he went up to his room. **g.** After living with her parents for two years, she rented a flat / apartment of her own in the city centre / town centre. **h.** Knowing how busy you are, I (have) filled in / completed the forms for you. **i.** Being a mother of four myself, I am very interested in this problem.

14N **a.** Are you interested in / Do you like adventure? **b.** Do you like travelling / to travel? **c.** with very good pay. **d.** What type / sort of work might the job offer / might it be? **e.** Why don't you become a member of our club? **f.** giving the details asked for. **g.** Some of my spare-time activities are. **h.** At the moment. **i.** give some more details. **j.** need. **k.** but not absolutely necessary.

14O **a.** People thinking of suicide. **b.** a girl to patrol the streets. **c.** anyone to look. **d.** old people living alone. **e.** A document saying. **f.** youngsters applying for work. **g.** sights to see. **h.** The woman showing. **i.** the things to look out for. **j.** a decent place to live. **k.** The lessons to be learnt. **l.** reading material reflecting. **m.** a salesman to sell. **n.** problems facing.

14P **a.** organized / offered. **b.** interested. **c.** likely; suitable. **d.** offered / described; involved. **e.** advertised. **f.** opened. **g.** found. **h.** used / found. **i.** named / called. **j.** parked / left. **k.** given / contained. **l.** shown. **m.** committed.

14Q For *some* years now I've *been* a member of a rather *unusual* kind of club. Time-Off Club, as it is *called,* helps you to spend your *spare* time as *meaningfully* as *possible* in the company of people *who* are interested in the same *activities* that you are interested in. For those *keen* on sport, for *example,* the club *organizes* ball games, *skiing* or mountain-*climbing* holidays, sailing or skin-diving *excursions.* If you *enjoy* just *meeting* people *socially,* they offer you parties, *eating* out, dancing, *discussions,* or *such* things. If you are *fond* of travelling, you can *spend* your weekends visiting interesting places, sightseeing, *walking,* hiking, *cycling,* or simply *relaxing* by the side of a hotel swimming pool. For members particularly *keen* on adventure, the club *organized* a trip *right* across the Sahara last year. There's always something *exciting* going on somewhere – Time-Off Club members never get *bored.*

15M Patricia has *won* a prize in some sort of competition, *hasn't she*? – Yes, she *has.* A week's *holiday* for two in Ireland. – For two? So she can *take* someone along on the trip. – Yes, a *friend* or relative or someone, whoever she *likes.* – *How* will they be travelling? – *By* train to London, and then *by* plane to Dublin. – But they won't be staying in Dublin all the time, *will they*? – No, of course not. They'll be *taken* round Ireland in a luxury coach, and there'll be a guide who'll *explain* / *show* everything to them. – And where will they *stay* / *stop* overnight? – At first-class hotels, in Killarney for *example* / *instance,* and in Limerick. – That *sounds* really splendid. And it's all free? – Yes. They'll even be *getting* seventy pounds spending money for the holiday. – Seventy pounds for each of *them*? – Well, I don't know. Maybe it's for the two of them *together.* In *any* case, that's pretty generous, *isn't it*? – It certainly *is.* When will she be *taking* the holiday? – I've no idea. She can go *any* time *between* the end of May and the middle of September. 15

15P Ireland is a republic *consisting* of 26 of the island's 32 counties – the other six *form(ing)* Northern Ireland, which is part of the United Kingdom. The Republic of Ireland *became* independent from Britain in 1921. The head of *state* is the President, but the leader of the government is the Prime Minister. The languages *spoken* in Ireland are English and Irish. A good restaurant meal *costs* about £7 in Ireland. If an Irishman *invites* you to a pub, it is normal for him to *buy* the first drink, after which you *buy* the next, and so on. In company, each member of the party is *expected* to buy "his" round of drinks. In conversation, the Irish like to *laugh* at themselves and their institutions, but they don't like strangers to join in.

15Q Ireland is an ideal *country* to spend a holiday. For *those* who like the *sea,* there are 3,500 miles of *coast* with a lot of *pleasant,* uncrowded *beaches.* The *countryside* with its *mountains,* lakes, and countless *streams* and rivers is *beautiful* and largely *unspoilt. Among* the many *tourist* attractions there are *castles,* cathedrals and other *historical* monuments as well as Ireland's *colourful* customs and folklore. For *those* keen on sports, there is tennis, *squash,* golf, riding and sailing; to the angler, Ireland offers some of *Europe's* finest fishing; for children there are *pony-trekking* holidays and many other ways to enjoy *themselves.* If you are *interested* in a holiday in Ireland, write to the Irish *Tourist* Board in Dublin, asking for a copy of *their* free *annual* brochure *Welcome to Ireland.*

15R **a.** by train; by plane. **b.** You will get a meal. **c.** parts. **d.** You will get £70 pocket money. **e.** You would have to leave Peterborough. **f.** answering the above letter / replying to the above letter. **g.** returned / got back. **h.** soon. **i.** She got home a little after / soon after.

15T **a.** 4. **b.** 3. **c.** 1. **d.** 4. **e.** 3.

16K **a.** different from theirs. **b.** and a few small ones. **c.** and so does my wife. **d.** even if I could. **e.** we won't be able to. **f.** anyone to look after the dog. **g.** companies advertising. **h.** before driving away. **i.** Being a mother of four. **j.** a competition run by *Holiday* magazine. **k.** something you shouldn't have missed. **l.** any cheaper ones. **m.** and so does Jack. **n.** the way you do. **o.** After studying. **p.** the kind of work they had been trained for. **q.** After eating. **r.** without putting. **s.** something he refuses to think about. **t.** than I do now. 16

16L **a.** She said in her statement that she'd been / that she had been on her way to work. **b.** The taxi driver said (that) he hadn't noticed the other car following him. **c.** She said (that) she had been driving for years and (that) she had never had an accident. **d.** The neighbours were surprised to hear that Mr Bates had left over £4,000 to his dog. **e.** Many people asked him where he had learnt / learned his excellent English. **f.** The policeman tried to find out how the accident had happened. **g.** The insurance company wrote me a letter asking what injuries I had received in the accident. **h.** She asked the attendant if / whether he had checked the oil. **i.** I was asked if / whether I had called the police. **j.** She asked Dick if / whether he had bought the scarf at Selfridges.

16N **a.** He was invited to supper / dinner. **b.** How were you treated in / at the camp? **c.** My car has been towed away. **d.** She was shown all the sights of Dublin. **e.** He was sent the free brochure *Welcome to Ireland.* **f.** English (is) spoken (here). **g.** People shouldn't be forced to wear seat belts. **h.** The following details should be noted down. **i.** The breeding, selling, and keeping of dogs should be controlled more strictly / more strictly controlled. **j.** Why couldn't the plans be changed / altered?

16O The experts tell us it's *wise* to *wear* seat belts when driving. Statistics *prove,* they say, that in most accidents you're much more likely not to get *badly* hurt if you're strapped to your seat and can't be thrown against the *windscreen,* the steering *wheel,* or some other *hard* part of the car. Motorists often *seem* to think it would be safer for them to be thrown out of the car in the *event* of an accident, but the statistics *leave* no *doubt* that being thrown out more than *doubles* the risk of being killed. An argument *often* heard is that in the *event* of the car *catching* fire, the people inside would be *trapped.* But *according* to the experts, this argument doesn't *hold* water: fire is *involved* in less *than* 1% of all accidents. And *even* if the car does *catch* fire, people strapped to *their* seats have a better chance of *survival* because the risk of *their* being *knocked* unconscious is much *reduced.*

17 17G **a.** We must prevent our customers (from) doing their shopping elsewhere. **b.** She said something about a policeman being very kind to her when she was all dazed and shaken. **c.** I saw a young woman being beaten up by a man in the street. **d.** What reason did she give for his / him taking up part-time work? **e.** Why is Malta so attractive a place in spite of its / it being so small? **f.** How can we prevent them (from) living in retirement towns like Worthing? **g.** Doesn't he mind their / them calling him Piggy? **h.** Everything now depended on our finding a suitable hotel. **i.** What was his boss's reaction to him / his setting up a business of his own? **j.** Don't you remember me / my mentioning his name? **k.** I can't imagine myself / me living in a bungalow in Spain.

17H **a.** It's supposed to be a very nice / pretty bungalow. **b.** Worthing is supposed to be a typical retirement centre. **c.** This book from the Pre-Retirement Association is supposed to contain a lot of important information. **d.** Seat belts are supposed to help most in head-on collisions. **e.** He's supposed to have gone to Spain. **f.** He's supposed to have said that the book was unsuitable for youngsters.

17I **a.** What caused her to write to a newspaper . . . What prevented her (from) writing to a newspaper . . . **b.** I encouraged him to take dancing lessons. She said something about him taking dancing lessons. **c.** I remember you / your checking the oil. I told you to check the oil. **d.** The landlord wouldn't allow them to keep a dog. The landlord wouldn't mind them / their keeping a dog. **e.** Fancy her going on holiday alone! I asked her to go on holiday alone. **f.** Would you like us to arrange accommodation? Would you mind our booking a room for you at a hotel? **g.** The policeman ordered the injured animal to be destroyed. The policeman prevented the injured animal from being destroyed. **h.** You're right about my / me being against the project. They hadn't expected me to be against the project. **i.** I'm against the retirement age being brought down from 65 to 60. I wouldn't like the retirement age to be brought down from 65 to 60.

17J *Thousands* of old people are living in *misery* in seaside towns to *which* they have *retired.* Pensioners who want to *spend* the rest of their *lives* in *peace* and *quiet* often find heartbreak *instead* as inflation eats away their *life* savings and they are left *lonely* and forgotten. In Worthing, for *example,* there are *6,500* old people who never *even* have a visitor. Worthing's medical and social *services* just cannot *cope* with the demands of the *60,000* old people who are now living in the *area.* There have *been* reports of old people never going out *because* of untreated *foot* problems, and of pensioners *wearing* someone *else's* dentures or glasses *because* they cannot get National Health *treatment* or *fear* they would be *unable* to pay *dentists'* bills. There are similarly *awful* conditions in many other seaside *resorts.* People *move* from industrial *areas* to the *coast* dreaming of a happy retirement. But things are *different* when they get there. Experts on retirement problems give this *advice:* Stay at home where you *belong* when the time comes to give up your job. Prepare *carefully* for retirement. Think of *worthwhile* hobbies and other activities that will *keep* you meaningfully *occupied.*

17K **a.** 2. **b.** 4. **c.** 1. **d.** 2. **e.** 2. **f.** 2. **g.** 3. **h.** 4.

18I **a.** (to) being. **b.** of being. **c.** at being. **d.** writing; filling. **e.** to retire. **f.** of finding. **g.** sitting. **h.** to bring. **i.** working. **j.** laughing. **k.** to let. **l.** to do / doing; studying. **m.** to hear. **n.** having. **o.** to causing. **p.** to give. **q.** seeing. **r.** to hear. **s.** of giving; starting. **18**

18J **a.** "If you take the holiday, you'll be sacked." **b.** "Mrs Green gave me only four days' notice that she intended to take the holiday." **c.** "The rule is for all the firm's employees to take their holidays at the same time." **d.** "This year in particular, exceptions can't be made because of the difficult economic situation." **e.** "I told Mr Wood about the holiday two weeks before." **f.** "My husband arranged the holiday as a surprise for me and didn't tell me too soon because he knows how excited I get."

18K *(Beispiele:)* **a.** Miss Wilkins told the tribunal that Mr Jackson had dismissed her on the spot. **b.** The chairman wanted to know why she had stayed away from work without asking permission. **c.** Julie told him that her fiancée had broken off their engagement three weeks before the wedding. She had gone on working until two days before the cancelled wedding but then felt she couldn't go on. **d.** The chairman of the tribunal asked her if she had tried to find another job. **e.** Julie Wilkins claimed she had applied for 45 jobs since her dismissal – with no success. (She said) She was quite sure (that) her dismissal had been counting against her. **f.** The chairman then asked Mr Jackson why he had dismissed Miss Wilkins without notice. **g.** Mr Jackson claimed that apart from staying away without permission, Miss Wilkins had frequently been late / had been frequently late for work and used bad language on the phone. **h.** Miss Wilkins was asked / The chairman asked Miss Wilkins if it was true that she had been late for work and used bad language on the phone. **i.** Julie explained that she had been late because of poor bus services during the holiday period. She had used strong language on one occasion when she was talking to her mother on the phone. **j.** The chairman of the industrial tribunal declared that none of the reasons given by the employer could justify instant dismissal. Miss Wilkins had been given no chance to state her own case, and that was completely against the law.

18L **a.** Is it really necessary for me to iron the handkerchiefs? **b.** Is it all right for me to take two days off this week? **c.** It would be understandable for him to be annoyed. **d.** It isn't normal / It's not normal for a dog to bite its / his own master. **e.** It's important for a secretary to look neat. **f.** The rule is for all the employees to take their holiday(s) at the same time. **g.** It isn't / It's not warm enough for the air conditioning to be turned on / for us to turn on the air conditioning.

18M **a.** consists of two people. **b.** When she got back / came back, she was sacked. **c.** When I returned / came back, Mr Jackson just didn't want to listen / just wasn't prepared to listen / simply refused to listen. **d.** Julie's employer . . . and used strong language. **e.** It is understandable that Mr Jackson was annoyed. **f.** I've got / I have a pain in my back. **g.** A holiday is quite impossible. **h.** She told her boss / employer only four days before / four days in advance that she was going to take / wanted to take. **i.** two weeks in advance. **j.** Other employees often got permission to take.

18N A 19-year-old dentist's *receptionist* who took two days *off* because she was upset *about* her wedding to a *soldier* being *called* off told an industrial tribunal in London yesterday that she was *dismissed* when she *returned.* Miss Julie Wilkins, of 4 Farm Street, W.1, was *awarded* £390 for unfair *dismissal* by Mr Kenneth Jackson, dental surgeon (= dentist), of 74 Harley Street, W.1. Mr Jackson's *secretary,* Miss Dorothy Young, said Mr Jackson told her to *dismiss* Miss Wilkins for being late, *taking* time *off* without *permission* and *using* strong *language* on the phone.

18O **a.** NT. **b.** NT. **c.** T. **d.** NT. **e.** NT. **f.** NT. **g.** T. **h.** T. **i.** NT. **j.** NT. **k.** T. **l.** NT.

19

19H **a.** Our children are expected to learn from us. **b.** Children are too often permitted to eat what they like. **c.** Our flat was broken into while we were away. **d.** She was given no chance to state her own case. **e.** I've been made organizer of the summer festival. **f.** A child had been heard calling from the flat. **g.** Other employees had often been allowed to take their holidays at different times. **h.** Exceptions cannot be made. **i.** This neighbourhood wouldn't be considered a very good place to grow up in. **j.** She will be provided with £70 spending money for the trip. **k.** This tooth will have to be filled, I'm afraid.

19I **a.** 4. **b.** 3. **c.** 3. **d.** 4. **e.** 4. **f.** 3. **g.** 1. **h.** 4.

19J **a.** Even the best driver may / can get involved in an accident. **b.** People might / could think I don't give him enough pocket money. **c.** They / You could now live / would now be able to live off the interest. **d.** They were now able to live off the interest. **e.** How could she do this to me? **f.** The child is afraid (that) someone / somebody bad might / could get into the house. **g.** May / Can I interrupt you for a moment? **h.** As children we were always allowed to eat / we could always eat what we liked. **i.** I had not been able / I had been unable to help him. **j.** I'm afraid we won't be able to come.

19K After *interviewing* 2,200 American children *aged* seven to eleven, experts have come to the *conclusion* that the kids feel *generally* good about *themselves,* their parents, and their *environment. According* to *data* published *recently,* the *vast* majority of American children feel happy about their families and *believe* their parents are *proud* of them. *Nearly* two-thirds of the kids say their parents *treat* them "more like grown-ups" than "like a baby". At the same time, *however,* the children show an *unexpected* fear of the *outside* world. More than two-thirds *report* that they are "*afraid* somebody bad *might* get into the house", *while* less than a third *regard* their own *neighbourhood* as "a very good place to *grow* up in". At *least* one in four *worries* that someone will *hurt* him when he *goes* outside to play, and the same proportion say they are *frightened* by *violent* programmes on television.

19L **a.** 1. **b.** 2. **c.** 1. **d.** 2. **e.** 3. **f.** 2. **g.** 4. **h.** 3. **i.** 2. **j.** 4.

20I **a.** is absolutely necessary. **b.** is certainly / really a wonderful idea. **c.** I thoroughly dislike. **d.** very relaxing indeed. **e.** certainly helps. **f.** extremely / terribly dangerous. **g.** There's really / certainly no need. **h.** he certainly didn't show it. **i.** is absolutely wonderful, and we are thoroughly enjoying ourselves / are enjoying ourselves thoroughly. **j.** He was in really high spirits. **k.** love you very much. **l.** completely lost. **m.** I'm terribly / extremely busy. **n.** Do you (really) think there (really) are people who can (really) predict the future? **o.** We'd very much like / really like / certainly like to see the film. **p.** very boring indeed. **q.** has certainly / really been improved / has been very much improved. **r.** it was absolutely / completely impossible. **s.** is (really) the only thing that (really) counts. **t.** It's terribly / extremely difficult. **u.** very unpleasant indeed. **v.** are really splendid. **20**

20J **a.** its. **b.** your. **c.** his. **d.** the. **e.** its. **f.** her. **g.** its / his / her. **h.** an / his. **i.** my; my. **j.** their; their. **k.** our. **l.** its. **m.** the. **n.** your. **o.** her.

20K **a.** She broke her contract (of employment) by taking a holiday without permission. **b.** There's a lot of money to be saved / You can save a lot of money by buying the jumbo size. **c.** The bus company is trying to keep fares down by reducing its services. **d.** The town fathers / city fathers solved the parking problem by having parking meters installed in the downtown area / in the city centre / town centre. **e.** He protests / is protesting against the fare increase by walking to work / going to work on foot. **f.** She improved her English by spending her summer holiday in England. **g.** He saved a lot of time by spending / staying the night at the airport hotel.

20L **a.** are unpleasant enough these days, when you think of / when you consider higher fares and exact money required. **b.** We really don't need the. **c.** pop music combined with commercials. **d.** I'm not surprised / It's not surprising (that) doctors' surgeries are crowded with people. **e.** an excellent idea. **f.** who dislike / don't like / can't stand. **g.** to get away from the music. **h.** that the majority doesn't mind / most of them don't mind the music. **i.** Maybe; provide; the ones. **j.** rise. **k.** I don't consider / find the music on the buses a bad idea. **l.** There's probably something in that. **m.** Anyone / Those / The ones / People who can't stand the noise ought to be provided with free ear plugs.

20M The important question is not *whether* the kind of music *played* on the buses is *acceptable* to passengers but *whether* we *should* allow *advertisers* to do what they have never *been* allowed to do before, that is, to *force* advertising on *people* who have no *possibility* of *escaping* it. Advertising is *often* annoying, but one can *always* turn a radio or television *off* or pay no attention to advertisements in the street or *elsewhere.* Against loudspeakers in a bus, *however,* one is *quite* helpless. The advertising *industry* is *quietly* trying to get the public to *accept* something new and *terrible.* In a *few* months we *shall* probably be told that the present ten minutes of advertising per *hour* is not profitable *enough* and that the proportion has to be *increased.* Then one morning we *shall* find loudspeakers at bus stops so that we can have the *pleasure* of *listening* to pop and commercials *while* we wait for the bus. The time to stop this nonsense is now. *People* must have the *right* to travel on a bus in *peace* and *quiet,* and the advertising *industry* and local *councillors* must not be allowed to *force* advertising on unwilling *victims,* and it *should* not matter *whether* a majority of sixty-five or a *minority* of five per cent of the population are against advertising on buses.

21

21H **a.** We do hope. **b.** I do understand. **c.** and he did escape. **d.** but they did finish it. **e.** It does sound strange. **f.** The book does contain. **g.** I do like. **h.** I do admit that I had a very lazy youth / I admit that I did have. **i.** does get on my nerves. **j.** but they did raise them. **k.** seat belts do make. **l.** does cost a lot of money. **m.** Do stop. **n.** Do be serious.

21I **a.** I'm puzzled myself. **b.** What do you think of it yourself? / What do you yourself think of it? **c.** Why not tell Inspector Raglan himself / yourself? **d.** Have you ever been there yourself? / Have you yourself . . .? **e.** Her mother educated her herself. **f.** that they try them out themselves. **g.** The music itself is not too bad. **h.** I was pretty badly injured myself. / I myself was pretty badly injured. **i.** I spoke to the murderer myself / himself. / I myself spoke . . . **j.** but they themselves are. **k.** We ourselves always wear . . . **l.** for the winning secretary herself. **m.** prizes for herself and her boss. **n.** and these are for ourselves.

21J **a.** which. **b.** –. **c.** that / which. **d.** which. **e.** who. **f.** whose. **g.** –. **h.** who. **i.** that / which. **j.** which. **k.** whose. **l.** –. **m.** whom. **n.** whom.

21L **a.** *The Murder of Roger Ackroyd* has become one of the most famous detective stories of all time. **b.** The older she gets, the more attractive she becomes. **c.** If he had gone to (the) university, he might have become / would perhaps have become an archaeologist. **d.** Your dinner / lunch / food is getting cold, Jack. **e.** It gets dark early at this time of year. **f.** I hope you('ll) get well soon. **g.** I'd get ill if I had to live in this house. **h.** That kind / sort of thing shouldn't be allowed. **i.** She was educated by her mother and could read at the age of four. **j.** Her first book was turned down by six publishers before a seventh published it in 1920. **k.** This / That film has been on / has been showing since the beginning of January.

21M Sir Max Mallowan, one of the *greatest* British archaeologists, *died* on August 19, 1978, *aged* seventy-four. Mallowan's first *wife* was Agatha Christie, one of the *world's* most *famous* and *successful writers* of detective *stories.* He met her *during* an expedition to Iraq and *married* her in 1930. Agatha Christie *accompanied* her husband on many of his expeditions and took a *keen* interest in his *archaeological* work. The *marriage* lasted over *forty-five / 45* years *till* Agatha Christie *died* at the *beginning* of 1976. In 1977, Mallowan *married* a second time, this time a *fellow* archaeologist. Mallowan was the author of *numerous* important *archaeological* works. His spare-time interests *included* gardens, *trees,* English *architecture,* and *travel.*

21N **a.** 1. **b.** 3. **c.** 4. **d.** 1. **e.** 4.

22

22G **a.** What (kind of) rights did America's blacks fight for? **b.** What (kind of) programmes are many children frightened by? **c.** What committee is Councillor Morris chairman of? **d.** What (kind of) reading material are parents suspicious of? **e.** What kind of toaster did the assistant recommend?

f. What (kind of) books are you interested in? **g.** What kind of hotel did you stay at? **h.** What kind of figure does the average American adult want? **i.** What kind of youth did he have? **j.** At what age did she die?

22H **a.** What time will they come? **b.** What date did they suggest? **c.** What company / firm does he work for? **d.** What subjects did he take A levels in? **e.** What kind of books / novels did she write? **f.** What kind of job does she have? / What's her job? / What does she do? **g.** What happened to the first book she wrote?

22I **a.** made; done. **b.** do. **c.** did. **d.** do. **e.** make. **f.** made. **g.** doing. **h.** do. **i.** made. **j.** does; does. **k.** making. **l.** do. **m.** does / did. **n.** made.

22J **a.** To own a car means to be free. **b.** To cook for him must be a pleasure. **c.** To abandon an animal is cruel. **d.** The worst you / one can do to a dog is to abandon it. **e.** My job is / It's my job to put coins in all the (parking) meters that are about to expire. **f.** Our greatest / biggest problem was to find a suitable flat / apartment. **g.** To be seventy years young is better than to be forty years old. **h.** To be, or not to be, that is the question.

22L *Between* 1930 and 1975 the black population in the U.S. *grew* from 9.69 to *11.48* per cent, and it is still *growing*. For someone looking at U.S. social *statistics* it is *easy* to see that blacks are an *under-privileged* minority. In 1976, the unemployment rate for *coloured* people was *almost double* that for whites. The unemployment problem was *especially* serious *among* young non-white workers: over 37 per cent of non-whites under twenty *were* out of work. Looking at the distribution of personal incomes one *finds* that non-whites outnumber whites by three to one in the *lowest* income *group* (under $3,000), while top incomes ($25,000 and over) are *mostly* earned by whites. The number of U.S. cities *governed* by black *mayors* has been *growing steadily* in *recent* years. The main *reason* for this *development* is that blacks have *increasingly* moved into the city centres while whites have moved out into the *suburbs*. *Since* the *majority* of people now living in the inner cities are not only black but also poor, *mayors* have their hands full *trying* to fight unemployment, crime, and the *growth* of slums.

23G **a.** 1. **b.** 2 / 1. **c.** 2. **d.** 1. **e.** 2 / 1. **f.** 2 / 1. **g.** 1. **23**

23H **a.** The Opposition are / is trying to undermine the welfare state. **b.** A new group of tourists has / have just arrived. **c.** The Social Services Committee are / is going to discuss this problem next week. **d.** The public is / are not prepared to accept another fare increase. **e.** The Government is / are considering a tax increase / an increase in taxes / raising taxes. **f.** His family were / was delighted to hear this news.

23I **a.** any. **b.** Someone / Somebody. **c.** anything. **d.** something. **e.** someone / somebody. **f.** anyone / anybody. **g.** any. **h.** any. **i.** some. **j.** any. **k.** anyone / anybody. **l.** any. **m.** Some.

23J **a.** You must not / mustn't misrepresent the facts. **b.** I must not / mustn't complain. **c.** We must not / mustn't let the murderer escape. / We must not / mustn't allow the murderer to escape. **d.** You must not / mustn't frighten the child. **e.** A court may order the destruction of an animal if it would be cruel to keep it alive. **f.** Up to the (nineteen) fifties, black children were not allowed to attend white schools. **g.** That should / must be the postman. **h.** That shouldn't have happened.

23L Fred O'Neill has not had a job for seven *years*. He was *thrown* out of work at the *age* of 32, and unless something very *remarkable* happens, he is not *likely* ever to work again. Every *Thursday* he *collects* his "wages", as he calls them, from a Government office; every *Tuesday* his wife *collects* the family allowance from another Government office; every week they and *their* five children are as *careful* as *possible* with the *money,* hoping that there won't be any unexpected *expenses.* The O'Neills live in a *council* house in a small industrial town in Cumbria, where the *unemployment* rate is three times the national *average.* There are jobs at the local labour *exchange,* but for Fred O'Neill they are *either* of the *wrong* sort or in the *wrong* place. He *refuses* to accept a job at less *money than* he gets on the dole because of the children. After *leaving* school, Fred had worked as a labourer for 16 *years* until *stomach* ulcers *forced* him to look for lighter work. He joined a Government *course* to be *trained* as a lathe operator and *then* quickly *found* a job. For the first, and *perhaps* only, time in his life he was *earning* good wages. *Within* three months, as a result of the *company's* financial *difficulties,* he *found* himself on the dole.

24 24H **a.** Mr Craig said (that) he'd build thc bungalow all the same. **b.** He claimed that the bungalow wasn't a bungalow at all but a stable. **c.** His neighbours asked him who was going to live in the bungalow. **d.** Old Harry said (that) the bungalow would serve as a stable for Ricky, his pony. **e.** The council inspector told Harry (that) it looked to him very much like a residential bungalow. **f.** The inspector asked Harry if / whether the living room with the fireplace was supposed to be used by the pony. **g.** Harry answered that the fireplace would be used for blacksmith work. **h.** The inspector wondered what the pony needed the fancy electric fittings in the bedroom for. **i.** Harry Craig said (that) the electric fittings were there in case the horse got ill and needed keeping warm. **j.** The inspector said (that) he thought Craig was just trying to get round the planning restrictions. He was afraid Craig's / the / his bungalow would have to be pulled down.

24I **a.** will he? **b.** didn't he? **c.** do you? **d.** doesn't it? / hasn't it? **e.** haven't you? **f.** isn't it? **g.** can't he? **h.** aren't there? **i.** hasn't he? **j.** would he? **k.** won't it?

24J **a.** don't like. **b.** I would be / I'd be. **c.** knew. **d.** I would be / I'd be. **e.** had. **f.** wouldn't have dismissed. **g.** would have been. **h.** I would have / I'd have wanted. **i.** he had / he'd fastened.

24L **a.** 4. **b.** 1. **c.** 3. **d.** 3. **e.** 4. **f.** 1. **g.** 1. **h.** 3. **i.** 3. **j.** 1. **k.** 4. **l.** 1. **m.** 1. **n.** 1. **o.** 3.

24M **a.** T. **b.** T. **c.** T. **d.** NT. **e.** NT. **f.** NT. **g.** T. **h.** NT. **i.** NT. **j.** T. **k.** T. **l.** NT. **m.** NT. **n.** NT. **o.** NT. **p.** NT. **q.** NT. **r.** NT. **s.** NT. **t.** T.

25 25H **a.** accompanied. **b.** made. **c.** wearing / dressed in. **d.** attracted; named / called. **e.** worn. **f.** built. **g.** inspecting. **h.** running / showing. **i.** attending. **j.** facing. **k.** given / printed / contained.

25I **a.** The money is to be used for a new iron grille. **b.** Although / Though great progress has been made, a lot remains to be done. **c.** The dog was nowhere to be seen. **d.** That was to be expected.

e. This / That question is to be discussed at the next meeting. **f.** There is no time to be lost. **g.** There was nothing to be done.

25J **a.** popular; popularly. **b.** surprisingly; surprisingly / enormously; surprising; surprising. **c.** badly; bad; badly. **d.** enormous; enormously. **e.** unconscious; unconscious. **f.** suspicious; suspiciously. **g.** irrational; irrationally. **h.** profitable; profitable. **i.** cruelly; cruel.

25K **a.** How long have you been married? **b.** How long have you known him? **c.** The Bible has been a best-seller for at least 450 years. **d.** This play has been on / has been running since last October. **e.** I've been driving / I've driven for years without an accident. **f.** We've been living / We've lived here for five years (now). **g.** Tell me, how long have we been sitting here? **h.** I haven't been feeling at all well lately. **i.** His girlfriend has been giving him the cold shoulder recently / lately.

25M San Francisco, *named* by the Spaniards after St Francis of Assisi, has a *pleasant* atmosphere *quite* different from that of *any* other American city. Its *youthfulness,* relaxed way of life and *beautiful* sights make it a *favourite* with both American and *foreign* visitors. The best *seasons* for *visiting* San Francisco are spring and autumn (*Herbst*). Winter is *relatively* warm, but in summer it can be *rather* cool when the late-afternoon *fog* comes in from the Pacific. One of San Francisco's *greatest* attractions are the cable cars, *which* are not only an *important* part of the *city's* transport system but also *provide* an easy and *exciting* way of seeing the *sights.* In 1906, an earthquake *accompanied* by fire *destroyed* the *whole* of San Francisco's central *area,* killing more *than* 500 people. *According* to recent *warnings* by experts, another – *possibly* even *worse* – earthquake could now *occur* at any time. The people of America's seventh largest city live *dangerously,* and they *know* it.

26

26K **a.** So you admit (to) stealing all the articles . . . **b.** She couldn't avoid telling her husband . . . **c.** The chairman began by asking her . . . **d.** He didn't dare to tell anyone . . . **e.** He had no difficulty (in) persuading the inspector . . . **f.** She enjoys reading detective stories . . . **g.** They went on protesting against . . . **h.** It had been her intention to write / She had intended to write / writing to the company saying . . . **i.** I'm looking forward to seeing you . . . **j.** She managed to convince them that . . . **k.** They made the mistake of buying a bungalow . . . **l.** He got permission to build a bungalow . . . **m.** He refused to pay the fine. **n.** I remember reading that book . . . **o.** She's right in believing that dividends . . . **p.** Stealing seems to give some people . . . **q.** I was shocked to hear that dog skins . . . **r.** It was difficult for them to find / They had difficulty (in) finding / They hoped to find / They managed to find / They tried to find / They were unable to find a flat in the city centre.

26L **a.** Where did she steal these things? **b.** What did she want to show? **c.** What did Mrs Fielding want to draw the company's attention to? **d.** How did Mrs Fielding want to draw the company's attention to shoplifting losses? **e.** Who stopped her? **f.** Who was she stopped by? **g.** When did the store detective stop her? **h.** Who has shares in Woolworth's? **i.** How many shares does she have in Woolworth's? **j.** How did the policewoman treat Mrs Fielding? **k.** Why do people steal?

26M **a.** I bought this at / in Woolworth's. **b.** Is it easy to shoplift in a store like Woolworth's? **c.** We always go to church on New Year's Day. **d.** We took / had a week's holiday at the seaside. **e.** We'll know more in a few days' time. **f.** It's about ten minutes' walk to the station. **g.** I met a friend of Jim's at the doctor's today. **h.** Do you know the Walkers' address? **i.** Are these typical women's occupations? **j.** Watching television / Watching TV is bad for young / small children's eyes / for the eyes of young / small children.

26N **a.** admitted (to) stealing; underwear. **b.** prove. **c.** I intended to write / writing / I was going to write; there had been (some) shoplifting at their Norwich branch so they would have to do. **d.** She has / owns shares in Woolworth's. **e.** sure / certain. **f.** I have to warn you that everything you say. **g.** Only very few of those caught. **h.** Do people find shoplifting exciting?

26P 22p store *thief* fined £50. A woman *who* stole a 22p tube of toothpaste was fined £50 by Norwich magistrates. Patricia Thompson, 54, of South Street, pleaded *guilty* to *stealing* the toothpaste from F. W. Woolworth in the High Street. Police Inspector Roger Wade, *prosecuting,* said that a security officer at the store *saw* Thompson take the toothpaste from a *shelf* and *put* it *into* her pocket. She *then* left and the security officer *stopped* her *outside.* Thompson told the magistrates, "I have never *done* anything like this *before.* I have not been *feeling* well for some time. I am *sorry.*"

27 27G **a.** fame. **b.** refusal. **c.** satisfied. **d.** robbed. **e.** inventor. **f.** admiration. **g.** deliver. **h.** calculated. **i.** unwilling. **j.** finger. **k.** piano; instruments. **l.** lamp. **m.** palace.

27H **a.** It was a boring / dull / an uninteresting match. **b.** Brazil was defeated by / beaten by England. / Brazil lost to England. **c.** shorter and less strenuous. **d.** failure. **e.** impolite / rude. **f.** winner. **g.** thinly. **h.** thin. **i.** untidy. **j.** Nobody / No one.

27I **a.** shortened / lengthened. **b.** loosen. **c.** widened. **d.** tightened. **e.** weakened; strengthen. **f.** sharpen. **g.** fastened. **h.** hardened / weakened / strengthened. **i.** softened.

27J **a.** success. **b.** controversial. **c.** they lost to / were beaten by. **d.** did not (manage to) beat. **e.** put the blame on. **f.** It's not the team manager's fault. **g.** We were beaten twice / lost two matches before we won our first match / had our first win. **h.** admired the team's successes very much. **i.** We expect delivery. **j.** invented. **k.** to be bank robbers. **l.** didn't want to help / weren't prepared to help. **m.** should be neat.

27L **a.** 1. **b.** 3. **c.** 3. **d.** 1. **e.** 3. **f.** 3. **g.** 4. **h.** 2.

27M **a.** NT. **b.** T. **c.** NT. **d.** NT. **e.** NT. **f.** T. **g.** NT. **h.** T. **i.** T. **j.** NT. **k.** T. **l.** T. **m.** NT. **n.** NT. **o.** NT. **p.** NT. **q.** T. **r.** NT. **s.** T. **t.** NT.

28 28K **a.** They let her sleep . . . **b.** They allowed her to sleep . . . **c.** They invited her to sleep . . . **d.** They didn't mind her sleeping . . . **e.** They didn't want her to sleep . . . **f.** He heard her cry(ing) for help. **g.** He prevented her (from) crying for help. **h.** He stopped her (from) crying for help. **i.** She didn't mind him / his drinking one or two . . . **j.** She didn't want him to drink . . . **k.** She got him to give up . . . **l.** I can't imagine him saying . . . **m.** She left him sitting on the ground. **n.** We saw a man beat(ing) up a young woman . . . **o.** He signalled me to remain . . . **p.** She remembered him / his putting the key . . . **q.** The robbers forced him to give them . . . **r.** She helped him (to) fill in the questionnaire.

28L **b.** She was allowed to sleep in the living room. **c.** She was invited to sleep in the living room. **f.** She was heard to cry for help. / She was heard crying for help. **g.** She was prevented from crying for help. **h.** She was stopped from crying for help. **m.** He was left sitting on the ground. **n.** We saw a young woman being beaten up (by a man) in the street. / A man was seen beating up / to beat up a young woman in the street. **q.** He was forced to give them all the money . . .

28M **a.** often break; suffer. **b.** is suffering. **c.** was working. **d.** work. **e.** certify. **f.** is improving. **g.** usually find; improves. **h.** is beginning. **i.** are having. **j.** have. **k.** were passing. **l.** shows. **m.** were sitting; were showing / sat; showed. **n.** am learning. **o.** learn.

28N **a.** so are. **b.** so am. **c.** so is. **d.** so was. **e.** so were. **f.** so do. **g.** so did. **h.** so have. **i.** so does / so has. **j.** so will. **k.** so could. **l.** so should.

28O **a.** So do I. **b.** Neither did I. **c.** Neither do I. **d.** Neither can I. **e.** So am I. **f.** Neither have I. **g.** So do I. **h.** So had I. **i.** So would I. **j.** Neither would I. **k.** So did I. **l.** So should I. **m.** Neither would I.

28Q RULES FOR GIVING UP SMOKING. 1. Always *refuse* a cigarette when it is *offered* to you – this weakens the influence other *people* have in *encouraging* you to smoke. 2. *Buy* one packet of cigarettes at a time, never more. 3. Every time you *buy* cigarettes, *buy* a different brand – this will weaken the hold a *particular* brand has on you. 4. Wait *until* after breakfast – or longer – before smoking your first cigarette. This will weaken the *daily* smoking routine you have fallen into. 5. Slowly *count* to ten before you light a cigarette. This helps to *break* the automatic actions you have *developed* over the years. 6. After each cigarette put the packet *away*. 7. If you run out of cigarettes, never let *anyone* give you one. 8. Slowly *increase* the number of places and situations where you don't smoke: *outdoors,* in bed, before meals, while driving, while watching TV, etc. 9. Always *keep* your cigarettes in another room so you have to make an *effort* to get them. 10. Never smoke a cigarette more *than* halfway down. 11. If you *want* a cigarette, wait five – ten – fifteen minutes before having one. 12. Never smoke *immediately* after meals; wait *until* you have left the table. 13. Don't smoke *while* you are waiting for someone or something. 14. When you smoke, stop doing all other things, i.e. do not watch TV, *read,* work, drink, etc. 15. Always sit on an *uncomfortable* chair *while* smoking.

29I **a.** You don't need to tell . . . **b.** I don't need to be told . . . **c.** You don't need to show . . . **d.** You really don't need to send . . . **e.** He doesn't need to help . . . **f.** We don't need to discuss . . . **g.** Does he really need to come back? **h.** Do I need to tell you anything else? – No, you don't. **i.** Does he need to put on a tie? – No, he doesn't. **29**

29J (In 29I *need* jeweils durch *have* ersetzen.)

29K **a.** achieved. **b.** has been divided. **c.** wants. **d.** have been; had claimed. **e.** was murdered. **f.** had been killed / were killed; threw. **g.** was announced; had dropped; compared; was; killed. **h.** killed; injured; were attending.

29L **a.** The number of smoking cars on underground trains is being reduced. **b.** Are these trousers being shortened or lengthened? **c.** The question of whether it was a goal or not is still being debated.

d. Black mayors are increasingly being elected. **e.** Her book is being made into a film. **f.** The firm my new book is being published by is in Vienna. **g.** The music that's being played on the buses seems to be acceptable to the majority. **h.** The bungalow that's being built up Thrush Lane is supposed to be a pony stable.

29 M **a.** The majority is / are in favour of Ulster remaining part of (Great) Britain. **b.** I remember him saying something about it. **c.** We must prevent it (from) happening again. **d.** Excuse my / me asking, but where did you learn your English? **e.** What (kind of) situation led to his / him treating the animal so cruelly? **f.** What was her reaction to his being promoted to (the rank of) lieutenant?

29 O Television has *changed* the world into one great *village.* People everywhere *know* what is happening everywhere else, they can watch it happen on *their* television screens in their living rooms. *Throughout* the western world people watch the same American-made *comedies,* crime *series,* thrillers, and Westerns. "Bonanza" and "Lassie" are *known* to hundreds of millions of people in about a hundred countries. In the *opinion* of many experts, British and West German television are among the best in the world. The TV *networks* of these countries are *praised* for the quality of *their* documentaries, plays, *news* magazines, and educational programmes. But even the best *networks* produce many *hours* of utter rubbish every day, and for someone who watches one of the more stupid programmes it is easy to understand why the TV is also *called* the "idiot box". Many people are *worried* about the effects of TV *violence* on children. One expert tells the story of a *six-year-old* boy who asked his father for *real* bullets for his gun because he wanted to kill his little sister "the way they do on television".

30

30 L **a.** Can you bring me the book? **b.** Can you bring me the book that's lying on the table in the living room? **c.** Can you give it to me / give me it / give it me? **d.** Can you give it to Jack? **e.** Can you give this book to the assistant who served us yesterday? **f.** I owe Jack £100. **g.** We owe this amount to Jack, not to the bank. **h.** She left all her money to the milkman. **i.** She left him a fortune. **j.** She left it to her son. **k.** He bought her a dictionary. **l.** He bought dictionaries for all (those) who needed one / them. **m.** He bought one for each / for every one of his children / each of his children one. **n.** He bought it for her / bought her it. **o.** Cook me one of your wonderful Chinese soups. **p.** He sold the trailer to a colleague who has a large / big family. **q.** Why don't you want to sell it to Jack? / Why won't you sell it to Jack?

30 N **a.** He showed her the house / showed the house to her. **b.** He described the house to her. **c.** He showed her the house that had been offered to him. **d.** He described to her the house that had been offered to him. **e.** Can you recommend us a hotel in Killarney? **f.** Can you suggest a better solution to us / suggest to us a better solution?

30 O **a.** very. **b.** very much. **c.** much. **d.** very. **e.** very. **f.** (very) much. **g.** very; very; very much. **h.** very. **i.** much. **j.** very much; very.

30 P **a.** get. **b.** Getting. **c.** getting. **d.** getting. **e.** get. **f.** gets. **g.** Getting. **h.** got. **i.** got. **j.** got. **k.** gets. **l.** get.

30 R **a.** 4. **b.** 3. **c.** 2. **d.** 1 / 2. **e.** 4. **f.** 1. **g.** 3. **h.** 1 / 4 / 3. **i.** 2. **j.** 1 / 4. **k.** 1 / 2 / 4. **l.** 3 / 4. **m.** 2. **n.** 1 / 3. **o.** 1. **p.** 3 / 1 / 4 / 2. **q.** 2 / 4.

Grammatikregister

Zur Erleichterung des Verständnisses der grammatischen Terminologie sind die in diesem Buch vorkommenden grammatischen Fachausdrücke lateinisch, deutsch und englisch mit Querverweisen aufgeführt.